Staying Sane

When You're
QUITTING
SMOKING

Staying Sane™
When You're
QUITTING
SMOKING

Pamela K. Brodowsky
Evelyn M. Fazio

Da Capo
∞
LIFE
LONG

A Member of the Perseus Books Group

Set in 12-point New Baskerville by the Perseus Books Group

Library of Congress Cataloging-in-Publication Data

Brodowsky, Pamela K.
   Staying sane when you're quitting smoking / Pamela K. Brodowsky,
Evelyn M. Fazio. — 1st Da Capo Press ed.
      p. cm. — (Staying sane series)
   ISBN-13: 978-0-7382-1034-6 (isbn-13; pbk. : alk. paper)
   ISBN-10: 0-7382-1034-X (isbn-10; pbk. : alk. paper) 1. Smoking cessation–
Popular works. I. Fazio, Evelyn M. II. Title.
   RC567.B76 2005
   616.86'506–dc22

                                                                2005020417

First Da Capo Press edition 2005

Published by Da Capo Press
A Member of the Perseus Books Group
www.dacapopress.com

Da Capo Press books are available at special discounts for bulk purchases in the U.S. by corporations, institutions, and other organizations. For more information, please contact the Special Markets Department at the Perseus Books Group, 11 Cambridge Center, Cambridge, MA 02142, or call (800) 255-1514 or (617) 252-5298, or e-mail special.markets@perseusbooks.com.

1 2 3 4 5 6 7 8 9—08 07 06 05

I am happy to dedicate this book with great love and affection to Carol and Lester Rowhwolt, and Win Huppuch—my three favorite ex-smokers. I also wish to dedicate it to the memory of Kim Cavellero and Rina Maiorano, two smokers whom I miss very much. Finally, to Pam, give it up already!

—Evelyn

This book is in memory of my father, whom I lost four years ago to an illness complicated by smoking. You are missed dearly every day of my life. My mother for never having smoked—two out of five isn't bad. My children, Sarah and Jacob, in hopes that you will never have to read a book on this subject. My husband, Edward, stop smoking, would you? And, Evelyn, I'll be outside.

—Pam

Contents

1

When You're Quitting Any Which Way You Can!

2

When You're Using Hypnosis, Acupuncture, and Drugs to Quit   45

3

When You're Coping with a Quitter   65

4

When You Fall Off the Butt Wagon   77

About the Staying Sane Series

The Staying Sane series is a collection of funny, irreverent, light-hearted, yet sassy, advice-laden books that are dedicated to finding the silver lining in the annoying, frustrating, or trying situations we all encounter every day.

The Staying Sane series shows you how to look for—and find—the humor and enlightenment in nearly every situation—you need only be open to seeing it. Let's face it: We all experience difficult times in our lives, and that's precisely why we've developed the Staying Sane series.

We want you to know that we've been through all kinds of demented things ourselves (oh, have we ever!), and we and our contributors plan to focus each volume on a specific topic to help you cope with some of the most typical—and most common— situations we all face at one point or another as we try to get through life.

Unlike any other books, the Staying Sane series' intention is to shed light on difficult situations, to bring laughter to people who are caught in a web of frustration and petty annoyances, and to provide help, advice, and answers for every situation; at the same time, we want to let readers know that they are not the only ones who've suffered through these irritating episodes or situations. Because laughter is truly the best medicine, the Staying Sane series will help you get through whatever comes up with as few dents and bruises as possible, and hopefully with your family re-lationships and friendships still intact when all is said (or not) and done (or not!).

Just hearing about other people's problems usually makes our own seem trivial by comparison, making us realize that things aren't really so bad. What's more, by reading about the scores of other people who've had the same or worse experience, we are able to get a more realistic perspective and regain our sense of proportion—all because we've been able to step back and see that things really could be much worse. And besides, misery loves company, doesn't it?

Staying sane isn't as hard as you think. Keeping it together when all hell breaks loose is just part of life—

something we have to do every day if we're living on planet Earth.

But one thing to keep in mind is that there is always someone else out there who is also on the edge of losing it. Our lives are complicated, but this doesn't mean we can't laugh at our problems—it can really help make them seem smaller and less overwhelming.

So when things are getting out of hand and you just don't think you can take it anymore, pick up a copy of one of the Staying Sane titles. It may be just what you need to keep from going off the deep end. We'll be right there with you, helping you cope!

Let Us Know

We would be delighted to hear your reactions to the stories in this and all Staying Sane books. Please let us know which stories you liked the most and how they related to your life.

Please send us your stories so we may share them with the world in future volumes of the Staying Sane series. Our email address is:

submission@staying-sane.com

You can also visit us on the Web at:

www.staying-sane.com

We look forward to hearing from you!

—Pam and Evelyn

About *Staying Sane When You're Quitting Smoking*

To find out how much you need this book, answer the following questions:

SANITY QUIZ

1. Does the thought of quitting smoking send you straight to your panic zone?
2. Do you find yourself cheating every time you try to quit?
3. Are you afraid to quit for fear of gaining weight?
4. Do you think trying to quit is just a waste of time?
5. Are you in fear for your life if you don't quit?

6. Will you go any distance or do anything for a cigarette?
7. Do you think your smoking doesn't matter?
8. Are your cravings unbearable?
9. Do you feel like telling the world to shove it?
10. Are you a closet smoker?

If you answered yes to even one of these questions, then you need to read this book! Find out how our contributors coped with the same problems, issues, and cravings you're experiencing as you try to quit smoking. They're the experts, so we'll let them speak for themselves!

When You're Quitting Any Which Way You Can!

Sanity Quiz

You have tried everything on the market to quit smoking: Zyban, Nicorette, the inhaler, everything, but nothing has worked. The next new product promising to produce successful results hits the store shelves.

Do you
A. run out immediately and purchase it
B. say to hell with it all, it's a bunch of bull
C. chalk it up to another probable failure and find your own way
D. go buy a pack of smokes instead

If you answered yes to any of these questions, you need advice, and fast! Read on to see how these successful quitters, these puffless pros, managed to get the job done.

Quittin' Ain't Easy!

Anthony Vlamis

WELL, I GAVE UP CIGARETTES about thirty years ago. But I can remember the pain and anxiety as if it were yesterday. I still suffer occasional relapses—you know, when you think you'd like to have just one big draw on a butt and savor the flavor. If God has a sense of humor, he or she will make sure that you cough your brains out for a solid five minutes, long enough to think you are about to aspirate your liver.

To give you some idea of my situation, I was a three-pack-a-day chimney who started smoking at thirteen; by the time I was thirty, I was so sick to my stomach most days that by the time I went to bed I had to lie down with one foot on the floor to stop the room from spinning.

Now, thirty years later, most of the time I find that cigarettes smell disgusting. But there is that once-in-a-while whiff of second-hand smoke that's almost intoxicating. And I guess that proves just how addictive nicotine is. After all, would you be likely to find yourself in bed with your ex-spouse thirty years after a divorce that was the worst time of your life? Hardly.

Now remember, I quit before the advent of acupuncture, nicotine patches, and nicotine gum. Even hypnotherapy wasn't available. And some of you out there might still want to do it the old-fashioned way. Either way, trust me: It is not going to happen overnight.

I tried cold turkey, but I felt like a pit bull in heat who just had his testicles waxed with hot pepper sauce. I would last a day or two until the sweats, shakes, and nico-visions (more like narco-visions) took over. And then I'd cave in. Or, as one of my friends would often say when I was so wired and irritable: "Tony, are you sure you want to do this? I liked you better when you were smoking."

Quitting the evil weed without losing your friends, coworkers, and significant other becomes a challenge. What a setup. You are trying to do something good for yourself by eliminating a life-shortening, love-aborting habit. If you don't think it's love-aborting, see how many smokers get hookups with nonsmokers. Did you ever really smell your breath after smoking a ciga-rette? Of course not. You can't smell it because the nicotine has dulled your sense of smell and your taste buds are just about useless for detecting anything but five-alarm chili. My teenage son smokes, as does more than 60 percent of the Gen Y population, but he has no idea how bad his breath smells; it's like a cross be-tween linoleum and cat gak.

Here's what got me through:

Have a Reason for Quitting.   Without a personal moti-vating rationale for ending the habit, you are just wasting time. It's like writing down goals. Okay, you don't want to hear another goal speech. Don't worry. I'm not giving it, but you have to have one sensible driving reason to focus on during those moments when everything is collapsing like a domino train. For me, it was breath. Or lack of breath. I was thirty-one years old and in otherwise trim shape, but I couldn't run half a block to catch the bus without feeling as if I needed EMS and the Externally Activated De-fibrillator. No kidding, I would be gasping and couldn't get enough air into my lungs fast enough. It felt like panic or as if someone had just put a plastic bag over my head. The point is that you won't succeed if you are quitting simply because your friends are doing it or there's a company campaign going on or your significant other thinks it's a good idea. Have your own personal reason or don't try at all.

Take It a Day at a Time.   Don't set a time limit for quitting. It's going to take you a long time to get there if you do. Think of dealing with your smoking habit today, one day only, and one day at a time. If you get through one day without a smoke, great. If not, start over tomorrow. And remember that you'll have cut down on your intake of toxic fumes and life-threatening carcinogens no matter what.

Change Your Behavior Patterns.   It's not just about the nicotine. It's about behavioral habits, too. Whenever I had a spare nanosecond of time, I'd automatically reach for the butts in my shirt pocket. So after a few weeks of this, I realized I needed to stop carrying my pack around when I left my desk. I left it in the desk drawer. Next, I moved it to a friend's desk. Reason: I had to ask my friend for a cigarette from my own pack. Finally, I stopped buying cigarettes for myself; instead, I would buy a pack and leave it with a coworker elsewhere in the office. By the way, resist the urge to bum cigarettes from smoking buddies. They'll soon be so annoyed with you that they'll start tossing you a pack of butts so that you'll get hooked again and stop the mooching. And if you won't listen to me on this score, at least have the good sense to buy your friend a pack of butts once a week.

When You Can't Stand It Anymore, Just Go Ahead and Have a Smoke.   Heresy, you say. No way. For the first several weeks, and maybe a couple of months, there were times when the craving for a butt was like an all-consuming lust. I felt like Ulysses, lashed to the mast and deprived of sex for six months and hearing the gorgeous breast-bared sirens calling to him with heavenly voices from the shore just beyond the impassable reef. For those of you too young to remember Ulysses, imagine it this way: I used to get a mesmerizing picture in my mind of a cigarette whisping smoke and, at that point, even in the middle of a conversation, I was transported to another place; it was as if Spock had put the Vulcan Mind Meld on me. When you get to that point, just cave in and go smoke a cigarette—just one, please. And then resume your penitent ways for another round. For me, the obsessive trances started to lessen, and eventually I could go a whole day or two without experiencing them. And getting the nicotine fix when I needed it kept me from eviscerating the first warm body in my path.

Avoid Affinity Situations. Did you ever notice how well coffee and cigarettes go together, or, worse yet, drinks at the bar and cigarettes? And after sex; well, let's not go too far here. The point is that for the first couple of months you need to stay away from situations and circumstances where a cigarette completes the picture for you. Try an Altoid mint after your cup of coffee. Or a change of venue for drinks. Anything that breaks the pattern.

Don't Quit Trying. It took me six months to quit smoking completely, and even then I sometimes was on the social cigar for another five years. This is not a transitory battle. It's an epic campaign that you must wage for the long-term. If you suffer a relapse, think of it as a setback but not the end of trying. Go back the next day and start again.

Believe in Yourself. Write on a Post-it note: "I Will Quit Smoking. I Will Beat This Habit." And look at it every-day. Even if you don't read it out loud, read it silently. And if you don't want to read it silently, just think about it. Do that and you'll make it.

I Was a Blind Smoker

Anthony Sommo

IT SOUNDS A LITTLE TOO MUCH like the title of a *Reader's Digest* article, but, yes, I was a blind smoker.

I stopped smoking when I was thirty-four, in 1981. I am, however, still blind.

In a short story by Raymond Carver, "Cathedral," a blind man named Robert visits an old friend who years before had volunteered to be his reader. The narrator, the former reader's husband, amazed that the blind man smokes, muses, "I thought that blind people didn't smoke because they couldn't see the smoke when they exhaled." Some motivation.

I started smoking when I was thirteen because I thought I was cool. It was the fall of 1960, four years before the surgeon general's report. A few months after I started, one day after school, I stood in front of Ivy Junior High in the Vailsberg section of Newark, pronounced "Nork" if you are from northern New Jersey. Two friends and I lit up on school premises.

A very proper English teacher, Mrs. Di Lessio, spotted us and said, "Boys! Put those cigarettes out immediately!" We just laughed and kept on smoking. "Well!" she said, "Tomorrow, I'm certainly going to report you to Mr. Siliano." That was the school principal. She fulfilled her promise. The next day, Mr. Siliano called us down to the office and suspended us for three days. In our adolescent minds, we had reached a new level of coolness. And I was *blind* cool.

Back in those days, smokers were divided into three categories: OPB smokers, who smoked "other people's brands"; smokers who smoked the same brand; and my category, smokers who switched brands. I was always trying different brands—filtered, recess-filtered, mentholated-filtered, unfiltered, and water- or charcoal-filtered to cut down on the tars.

We bought into what the ads told us—that filtered cigarettes were not as harmful to your health. We called certain brands "cancer sticks," which, of course, implied that others were not. When I was bored, I would, on occasion, rip the filter from the rest of the butt after I had finished a cigarette and check to see if there really was water or charcoal inside the filter. The tobacco companies were telling the truth—at least about what was inside a filter.

Throughout adolescence, I kept this do-it-yourself mechanical device, pouches of tobacco and Zigzag papers with a strip of glue at one end, and rolled my own. More blind coolness. These smokes were okay on the pinch, but the tobacco was strong.

I went from smoking because I was cool to a nasty habit that lasted twenty-one years. I tried to quit any number of times; sometimes I might be off the nicotine for six, seven, or eight days. Then I gave into the urge and went back.

I remember feeling dizzy smoking that first cigarette of relapse. I would excuse the weak-kneed feeling by telling myself that my body would adjust.

In 1981, I quit on a dime. At the time, I was a graduate student in sociology at the University of Connecticut, and I spent much of the time playing cards with Gerry and Trudi, the owners of Huskey's Bar and Grill. Of course, I used brailled cards. My fellow players accused me of cheating all the time. Not so. I just beat them at crazy eights, gin, and poker. My last brand was Moore's, and the cigarettes resembled thin brown cigars. I, apropos of nothing, just quit.

Chiclets served as my substitute addiction. Boxes and boxes of Chiclets. Now that I think about it, Chiclets was an arbitrary choice. Why not root beer barrels? I can't say.

For the next three months, I would go to this bar and that and derive vicarious pleasures from snorting secondary smoke; but I felt no temptation to return to the habit. I was done. The negatives outweighed the plusses. At thirty-four, being cool was not a high priority. I hated smoke-phlegm breath in the morning. And I now could taste food as food.

Thinking about it now, I remember that the best thrill I got from smoking was a cup of coffee and a cigarette in the morning. Last week, I was visited by an absurd thought: I haven't held a book of matches in years. For some reason, as part of my own personal mythology about cigarette culture, I concluded that people who used cigarette lighters were not as cool as people who struck matches.

SURVIVAL HINTS

1. Stop smoking.
2. If you're not puffing on the weed already, don't start. It's as simple as that.
3. If you do smoke and you want to quit and stay that way, chew gum to keep you from missing a cigarette in your mouth.

Smoke Gets in Your Sighs

Edward F. Fitzgerald

FEW THINGS ANNOY ME MORE than the idea that one has to resort to extraordinary measures to perform a simple act such as quitting smoking. Excuse me a moment. I apologize. I'll be right back.

> Doctor!
> Do you mind? I'm in the middle of something, as you can plainly see.
> Please! Just be patient for a moment.

I do not easily get upset or rattled, but I confess that something akin to a smoldering rage does suffuse me when people suggest that quitting smoking is extremely stressful, possibly even psychologically damaging if not handled with care and caution, and that perhaps medical advice may be needed. Nonsense! Absurd. Nothing could be simpler, in fact, for a man or woman of character, one with a reasonable sense of discipline, than to . . .

Now, look, Doctor, I think I asked you quite nicely to give me a few minutes here and I . . . excuse me? Where did I get the pen? Well, surely, you didn't really expect me to write an important document with that stubby crayon the nurse gave me? Alright, okay, if you're going to have these two pug-uglies manhandle me, I suppose you can have the damn pen. Now just ask them to put me down and I'll take your rotten pills, but in the name of God just give me one lousy weed first!

Well, all right, let's be honest. I didn't *really* end up in the Arizona Home for the Perpetually Bewildered when I quit smoking—it only felt as if it could happen to me at any moment—at least for a while it did. Because, indeed, as you smokers know, trying to quit smoking can be maddening—a bit like prepping your own molar for a filling using a hand-drill. However, it can be done—yes, it can—if you understand and follow the few simple principles I have outlined here.

Change Your Routine and Habits.   If your breakfast usually consists of coffee, cigarettes, and the morning newspaper, have tea instead with a good Charles Dickens novel; and instead of smoking, practice saying out loud the new words and phrases you may have picked up. ("I say, old chaps, this is bloody revolting, eh, wot?") If you usually have a leisurely smoke after dinner, jump up instead, dash outside, and enjoy a bracing twelve-mile jog before retiring. You'll still want a cigarette when you finish, of course, but washing the blood out of your socks and pricking the blisters on your heels will tend to keep you otherwise occupied.

Avoid Smokers, Associate with Nonsmokers.   Needless to say, smokers will hate your guts for quitting anyway, and they'll loathe your endless prattle about how great food tastes now, and how sweet it is to breathe fresh air. They will avoid you as though you were Osama Bin Laden at a christening. And the nonsmokers are always easy to find. They will be the ones with their heads tipped back, staring down long noses at your nicotine-stained fingers and making the sound Joe Palooka used to make in the comics (tch, tch)—and if you remember that, you've already been smoking far too long.

Find Satisfying Oral Substitutes.   Be aware that the continuous need to place things in your mouth will not stop when you quit. Lifesavers, chewing gum, candies of all types, brownies, whole pies, barrels of M&Ms (you think I'm kidding, but just you wait). Or you can be more imaginative and roll other types of things around in your nicotine-stained teeth in your angry, disgruntled mouths. Celery stalks are good. Leeks, even. Carrots, rhododendrons, flowering hibiscus, small pine trees. Note: Rolling red cabbage in a limp lettuce leaf and torching it when your spouse steps out of the room is an unacceptable substitute (and the ashes also set my shirt on fire).

Cut Back First, Quit Second.   Before you quit, taper off. First go from three packs a day to two, then to one, then to six cigarettes a day, then to three. After a week of that, don't be surprised by how easy it is—to end up backsliding, then to end up smoking four packs a day instead of the original three! (Hey! No one said this would be easy.) However, if you find yourself constantly reverting back and having to start over, then it is time to bite the bullet and do it cold turkey. See below.

Quit Cold Turkey!   Ever wonder why they call it that? The first time your significant other disappears into the kitchen after dinner and you find yourself lighting up one of those meaty drumsticks, you'll understand.

People who do this are easy to recognize, and to flee from. Keep in mind that it is this group who taught us the meaning of the term "primal scream." But above all else, remember the following.

You Will Quit When You Are Ready to Quit and Not Before.   It has been noted by psychologists that in the final analysis smokers quit only when they are physically and mentally ready for this major upheaval in their heretofore pleasantly decadent lives. Moving across the line from smoker to nonsmoker does signal a "sea change" in our appreciation of the "pleasure-pain exchange principle"—when certain simple pleasures are given up now to avoid a greater pain later.

So how does one at long last come to realize that smoking is not all it has been, uh, puffed up to be? For the husbands among us, the decisionmaking process is greatly simplified. Our wives tell us when we are ready to quit. For married women, your husbands will tell you when you are ready. As for you singles—smoke this!

But I jest. The fact is that I had never realized until I quit what a filthy habit smoking really is. I don't say that to offend anyone, but it is the simple truth, one that even smokers recognize when they think about it. Filthy in every sense of the word. In the nose-crinkling miasma left behind wherever smokers have been. In our fouled breath. In the defiled atmosphere that our friends and loved ones must breathe. In the ineradicable stink that seeps into our furniture, curtains, and clothing, remaining long after our temporary fires have been extinguished. And in the disgusting refuse of our discarded "butts" piling up in ashtrays and littering our yards and highways.

I quit in 1974, by the way, a long time ago now, and I want you to know that I don't miss it for one minute—an hour here and there, yes. Still, I am glad I quit and I never look back with regret. What's more, I promise you that if you just pull yourself together and do it, if you once and for all take that giant, all-important step, you will never regret it, either. I promise you that on my mother's grave. And on the box of stubbed and crumpled Marlboros I keep under the bed and that I still dig out and sniff in the dead of night. Hey! I didn't create the concept of the addictive personality, guys—I just live with it!

Edward F. Fitzgerald is the author of the humorous novel *Bank's Bandits: The Untold Story of the Original Green Berets* (of which he was one).

Farewell to the Marlboro Man

Theodore Pollack

I'LL TELL YOU A SECRET.

There are a dozen remedies now widely available to help you quit smoking. Everyone knows about the patch and the gum, and most people are familiar with the inhaler. There's also a drug called Zyban, which is really just another name for Wellbutrin. For a while, I worked in a drugstore that sold nicotine-laced bottled water. I'm not sure whether switching to that is a super health move or just a sign of insanity.

The point is, there's only one way to quit smoking.

Three years ago, I spent six months using the patch. I used the one that allows you to step down from strong patches to weak patches. And it worked. Between the constant nicotine supply and the warning on the label that sneaking a cigarette could cause a stroke, I didn't take a puff the entire time.

And for six months, I wanted a cigarette.

It wasn't like when you first stop smoking, when you're absolutely dying, when all you can think of is slinking out onto the fire escape and sucking down a smoke. Just one, of course, and then you'll quit again. It wasn't bad like that. But it never went away. Every night I went to bed proud of myself for not smoking, and every morning I woke up wanting a cigarette.

It was always an issue.

After six months, I'd had enough of the patch, and I cut myself loose. For the next few weeks, I was a total bastard. I cursed at strangers. I refused to smile. I didn't sleep for days at a time. Finally, I caved in and smoked a cigarette. It made me cough, like the first cigarette I'd smoked, at age fifteen. But I became human again. I could laugh at myself. I could smile.

And I could sleep.

Needless to say, I was back to a pack a day in about two weeks. It took me another year and a half, and developing asthma, to quit smoking again. I knew I had to stop, but the memory of quitting with the patch was a bad one. Finally, the combination of coughing and wasted money pushed me over the edge, and I said good-bye to the Marlboro man for a second time.

Hello, patch.

This time, I seemed to develop some kind of allergic reaction to the thing. The backs of my hands started itching like crazy, and I was guzzling water from dawn to dusk. I switched patch brands, but eventually the new patches started causing their own strange symptom: My ribs were always sore. I was sure I had smoked for too long, and that I was dying, at twenty-three, of some horrible, cigarette-related illness. I went to the doctor; he ordered a bunch of blood tests and assured me that I was healthy. I didn't touch a cigarette for two months.

Then I met a girl who was a smoker.

I held out for two weeks, maybe three, but soon we were spending a lot of time together. One thing led to another, and I was smoking again. But at that point, I knew my days as a smoker were numbered, and I started smoking like a chimney. At the end of the summer, the smoker girl went her way, and I went mine. I was determined, then, to stop smoking once and for all.

I used the patch once more for what it was good for: breaking the hour-to-hour physical habit of smoking. It really is easier to deal with the habit and the nicotine issue separately. I used the patches for a week. Once I stopped reaching for my lighter every time I walked out the door, I threw the rest of them away.

The point is, there's only one way to quit smoking.

For the next few weeks, I drank a lot of green tea. And I was a total bastard again. Cursing, scowling, and sleepless. But the misery was at the outset of the process, not after six months' effort. I'd wasted enough money, worried enough about my health, and I resented the feeling that something was controlling my behavior. So I put up with the misery for a while longer. Slowly, my normal personality came back.

And then something amazing happened. One day, after about a month of drinking tea, I realized that I didn't want a cigarette. In six months of using the patch, that had never happened.

These days, I still think about how I liked to have a cigarette in certain situations: when I was walking down the street in New York City; when I was writing; after a good meal; with a drink. It's in those situations that I still think of smoking, and I still miss it. And when life is stressful, I miss being able to take a break and light up. But it's more of a nostalgic feeling than a compulsive urge.

I've known people who've used the inhaler, the gum, the pill, and the patch, and I haven't heard many success stories. All I know is that I quit for six months without any special remedies, and I think about smoking a lot less now than I did after six months on the patch.

So that's it. There's only one way to quit smoking: You just stop. And sometimes you have to do it more than once. And it really, really sucks. But I imagine it's easier, and definitely saner, than some of the alternatives. Like nicotine-laced bottled water.

SURVIVAL HINTS

1. Accept that you might be grumpy, short-tempered, and not yourself for a while.
2. There are many different techniques for quitting, and it's okay to try more than one.
3. Don't be surprised if it takes you more than one attempt to quit.
4. Be persistent, because there's really only one way to quit—just do it!

Frozen Addicts: How They Helped Me Quit Smoking

Jenks Martin

GALLION, OHIO, WAS MY HOME until last year. I had spent thirty wonderful years there. Ohio has been one of those Midwestern states where smoking was generally accepted. Bars, beers, and a pack of cigarettes were as Ohio as corn and tomato juice. Most of my friends in my hometown smoked, and I thought nothing of it other than something that adults were privileged to do, even though I started my habit as a teenager.

When I was approaching thirty, jobs and opportunities were becoming hard to come by in Gallion, especially for upwardly mobile adults like me, so I found a good job in Ohio's capital and largest city, Columbus. Even though Columbus is only an hour's drive from Gallion, I discovered during my job interview that smoking and smokers are looked upon much differently down there. In Columbus, antismoking activists had gathered enough signatures to place one of the strictest antismoking laws in America on the local ballot. The initiative was called the Clean Indoor Air Law and it was even stricter than similar laws in California and New York.

My start date at my new job in Columbus was the week after the no-smoking law passed by a wide margin, banning smoking in public places such as restaurants and (astoundingly) bars! With a two-pack-a-day smoking habit, and long being accustomed to an after-work drink in a favorite watering hole, I found it hard to imagine sitting on a stool drinking a beer without a cigarette. Even more unbelievable, the new law forced smokers off the sidewalks because it banned smoking within twenty feet of buildings. In Columbus, not only did you not have the freedom to smoke in a bar, you could get ticketed for walking down the street carrying a lighted cigarette. I felt as if I had moved to a totalitarian state.

My new favorite after-work hangout in Columbus was on High Street, the main drag. It had great wings and even better draft beer. Luckily, because of the smoking ban, I made instant friends, other smokers who joined me for a mid-beer smoke break several times each evening. A bunch of us would light up, talk, and smoke illegally on the sidewalk. Everyone knew that the local police were not going to ticket sidewalk smokers in the first weeks, and besides, it was cold, and we were outside, after all.

As a joke, and perhaps to show off a bit to make friends, I would step off twenty feet from the front door, marking the legal smoke line away from the buildings. Everyone found this very funny because I ended up standing dangerously close to High Street traffic, all just to smoke. Sometimes others would join me for a "legal smoke," and it helped me break the ice with more people than I'd ever imagined.

December is cold in Columbus. After a couple of weeks of gaining a reputation as the legal smoker, I had a fortunate but painful revelation. I realized something about smokers that I had never really noticed before. One night, with a slight beer buzz, I lit my cigarette in the street and turned back toward the sidewalk. About twenty smokers huddled on the sidewalk, shivering in the rain/snow mix and quickly sucking down their cigarettes so they could return to the bar's warmth. The sight was like a scene from a movie: a pathetic, low-budget B-flick.

These people were addicts, braving the wind and weather, standing around like crack heads, administering their drug, getting their fix, and reaping scorn from a huge majority of Columbus voters. Here I was, forced to the street to keep myself high, perhaps even more pathetic than the other poor nicotine addicts puffing on their drugs. I watched four of my new acquaintances take up most of the sidewalk as they stood in a circle. Ordinary pedestrians slinked around them on the sidewalk's edge, and I could see how horrified they were, some even visibly holding their breath before emerging back into the fresh air beyond the circle. The addicts, oblivious to their own rude behavior, concentrated only on getting the most out of their fixes.

I kept watching in horror as the smokers used the street as an ashtray. A few shivering addicts eventually went back inside, but new addicts joined the crowd, hogging the sidewalk, devouring their drugs, and huddling together in the cold. It was a merry-go-round of addicts. I stayed in the street watching this movie for twenty minutes, and some of the addicts even returned for another hit. Lit cigarette butts continued to fly in the air, exploding on the pavement. The film, *Frozen Addicts*, might never have ended if I hadn't gone home.

Even with my two-pack-a-day habit, I decided to quit smoking that night. It's been six months since the movie debut, I've been through hell, I've spent hundreds of dollars on patches and gum, and I'm down to half a pack today. I'm giving myself six more months in which to succeed, and I will.

The withdrawals are still painful and extremely uncomfortable, but I refuse to be the star of a B-movie. For the smokers out there who really want to quit smoking, I recommend voting for legal bans on smoking in public places. Then the addicts come out into the open. If you are like me, you might not want to join them.

SURVIVAL HINTS

1. Sometimes you have to step back and be objective to see how crazy smoking behavior can be. It's not really worth all the inconvenience, is it?
2. If you can restrict yourself to places where you can't smoke, you'll be able to cut down even before you actually quit.
3. Support local legislation to ban smoking. The fewer places where you're exposed to people who smoke, the better. Decreased exposure will keep you from temptation, and you'll be less likely to want a cigarette.

How I Quit and Stayed Smoke Free

Nidal Awad

I QUIT SMOKING for a lot of reasons, but the main one is my children. My wife and I have four; two boys, two girls, ages four to fourteen. They are the joy of our lives.

On May 31, 2004, my youngest son's birthday, I called him to tell him that I was quitting smoking for his birthday. He was very happy, and so were the other three kids. They want to make sure I'm around and healthy as they grow up, and so do I.

I started smoking when I was thirteen. My older brother had started smoking, and I used to be his lookout when he snuck out for a smoke. As payment, he would give me a couple of drags on his cigarette. And that's how my habit began.

I come from the Middle East. Everyone there smokes. It's not easy to be the only nonsmoker when I go home for a visit. It's a long flight—twelve hours— and when I smoked, going for that length of time without a cigarette was difficult. But more than a year ago when I made that trip, I realized that if I could go twelve hours without a cigarette, then I could quit, and shortly after that trip I did.

Recently, my mother had a stroke, and I had to go back to see her. When I went home this time, after having quit for almost a year, I was concerned that I wouldn't be able to avoid smoking considering the stress and the fear about my mother's condition. Not only that, but everyone else was smoking constantly, and we were huddled in small enclosed hospital waiting rooms for much of the time. It was tough because not only did my entire family turn out to wait at the hospital, but most of our neighborhood as well— everyone back there is very close—and every last one of them smoked the whole time.

You might wonder whether I craved a cigarette then. My body did; I felt itchy, but I endured the smoking around me without caving in. When I came home from the hospital each night, my clothes reeked of smoke. My wife hung them outside to air, and I hated going back to those smoky places day after day, but I still didn't smoke. My father and brother never believed I'd make it—they just didn't think I could quit. But after this visit, and especially after those hospital visits, they know I mean business.

Another reason I quit was because of my job. I'm the security captain who guards the door of a high-rise condominium, and smoking isn't allowed inside the building's common areas. Residents may smoke in their apartments, but nowhere else. That goes for the lobby, and the guy who works there, too. That's me. I stand or sit in the lobby for eight or nine hours a day, and because I can't smoke while I'm there, it was easier to quit.

When I smoked outside the front door, people upstairs complained. So I was relegated to the back room, by the garbage compactor. One day it became clear to me: I am paying seven dollars a pack to smoke next to the garbage. Am I crazy? That thought kept me motivated to quit, right along with the promise I'd made to my kids.

This may sound strange, but when I quit, I kept a pack of cigarettes and a lighter on the nightstand by my bed. Every morning when I got up, for the first seventeen days of quitting, I spat at that pack of cigarettes. I'd still be doing it, but my brother came to visit and he swiped the pack and the lighter. Little does he know what I'd been doing to them! I guess he'll find out when he reads this book.

The final reason I quit was money. It just got too expensive—which I guess was the point of raising the prices. Since I stopped smoking, nearly a year ago, I've saved more than eighteen hundred dollars. That's a lot of money, and I use it for my kids. Whatever they want, I buy it for them, and it's all thanks to not smoking. If they need a computer, if they need shoes, if they want a toy or a doll, all they have to do is ask and the money is there for them.

Cigarettes took advantage of me for twenty-three years. Nobody stopped me at home because it's part of the culture of the Middle East. Even when I started working at this job seven years ago, the residents brought back cartons for me from the duty free shops when they traveled, and sometimes they'd just give them to me as a gift or a tip. Now I keep a few packs around—just in case one of my residents runs out or is desperate, but they hold no appeal for me. Now they're just here for other people's emergencies, not mine.

Now that I no longer smoke, people tell me how well I look. My skin isn't pale, and there's color in my cheeks. I don't get out of breath anymore, and I feel so good all the time. Now I don't smoke when I wake up in the morning, I don't smoke before brushing my teeth, and I don't smoke before meals. I'm free and I'm happy. So I've gained a few pounds—it's nothing to worry about, I'll walk it off on the job. It was absolutely worth it.

As I said, I want to be here for my children. I want to spend all my money on them. Every day I put five dollars in a piggy bank, just for them, to buy things they need, and all from the money I save from not buying cigarettes!

SURVIVAL HINTS

1. When you first quit, avoid going to places where people smoke so that you are not tempted to join them.
2. Try to find a compelling reason that means something to you when you're trying to stay away from cigarettes. It could be health, money, or someone else's need—whatever will motivate you to stick to your plan.

Quitter's Flu

Peter Mastracchio

SMOKERS KEEP HALF A DOZEN reasons for quitting close to their hearts at all times. My story begins when it was finally my time to quit and I needed to pick one of those reasons. Could my reason weather the storm of quitting and last me a lifetime? I imagined a helpful stranger (probably an ex-smoker) spinning a carnival wheel imprinted with those reasons instead of the usual numbers and symbols. We all daydream crazy ways around our most difficult choices. The wheel spun and clicked ever more slowly until it stopped on one of them. For me, twenty years ago, it was personal hygiene. Not very dramatic, but I was happy to have the torment of picking a reason behind me. There was no life crisis, no sudden enlightenment; I was ready, and that reason was as good as any.

In the weeks leading up to my last cigarette, I had an abiding sense of feeling dirty all the time. My clothes, hair, fingertips, and all my pores seemed to ooze an odor that was tart and suggestive of brownish yellow. Showers washed away the surface film only. Long, soaking baths helped, but only for a while. Half an hour in a sauna drew the toxins out of me and let me feel clean the longest.

I had quit many times before. Each time I experienced a sample of nicotine withdrawal, but never in its full fury. And I had never quit long enough to experience something called "quitter's flu," which is a collection of symptoms that the antismoking folks like to sweep under the rug. It seems that after you stop coating your mucous membranes with tar and other chemicals, something life-affirming happens right away: All your cilia (which are self-propelled scrub brushes located throughout the respiratory system) finally wake up and do their job. Unfortunately, the accumulated gunk doesn't just evaporate or dissolve into the bloodstream. The cilia need help and demand months of strenuous coughing, throat-clearing, and spitting. I imagined another necessary warning imprinted on cigarette packs: "Smoker *will* break up and spit out tar, at great cost in energy and dignity." So it was ironic that cleanliness, which I gratefully accepted as my very own reason to quit, would cause such dirty and disgusting side effects.

I don't really remember experiencing the other, more well-known nicotine withdrawal symptoms: headache, difficulty concentrating, irritability, and all the rest. If I experienced any of them, they were fleeting—the occasional dark clouds on sunny days. Quitter's flu was the protracted rainstorm.

Personal hygiene wasn't the only reason I quit. There was another, more sinister motivation—another spin of the carnival wheel just in case the first reason didn't take hold. This time, it landed on "self-doubt." I started to wonder whether I could accomplish anything really difficult. Of course, the whole world was against me during this time. I was near the end of a master's degree in computer science and my grade point average was hovering just below 3.0. The dean explained that I couldn't graduate if my average was lower than 3.0 and questioned whether I had the resolve to finish what I had started. I'm sure she had no idea that I was already asking that question myself. To get even, I pictured her wearing a clown suit and spinning a carnival wheel.

Antismoking literature claims that the symptoms of quitter's flu are usually mild and last from a week to a couple of months at most. The fine people who write those materials don't want to scare anyone away from quitting. In fact, their claim is true for most people who quit. My quitter's flu lasted six miserable months, and then left me—as suddenly as a demon departing after an exorcism. The experience is a distant memory now. Whenever it comes to mind, I remember it as one of my best bargains—six months of discomfort for twenty years of feeling clean and knowing that I finished something that seemed impossible at first. If you quit, you will probably brush aside quitter's flu, or perhaps never experience it at all. But the unvarnished truth with all its bumps and fake-outs is the best way to approach anything difficult, especially quitting smoking.

Quitter's flu brings hoarseness, postnasal drip, and a "productive" cough (as if something valuable were being created or discovered). For me, the flu symptom was the almost constant sensation of mucous flowing through an open faucet and tickling my gag reflex. It ceased only long enough to give me the chance to cough up whatever had dripped into my lungs. The mucous wasn't benevolent and lubricating, but caustic; it left me speechless most of the time. I resorted to head-nodding and one-syllable pronouncements in my efforts to appear authoritative with my spare answers. I dreaded classes and business meetings because that's when the worst of it usually struck and I would inevitably be asked to *say* something!

In addition to attending graduate school, I was working as a computer operator during those six months. One day, my manager decided to try out the latest technology, a modem that would connect our computers in Greenwich, Connecticut, to computers in the Manhattan branch office. It was 1984, and in those days such an idea was considered a wild scheme. I don't think the boss knew anything about my fragile emotional and physical state. Nevertheless, he dispatched me to Manhattan to hook up the modem and explain how to operate it. Under the best of circumstances, without my quitter's flu, the assignment would be akin to a missionary trying to convert savages to Christianity.

Sure enough, the folks in the branch office were flabbergasted by what I wanted to do. "Let me get this straight. You want to hook up our computer to the big one in Greenwich over the phone line?!" I really don't blame them for being skeptical. I was asking them (none too eloquently) to abandon old and reliable office routines. In truth, the once-a-month phone call between secretaries to exchange sales totals was far more practical. When I started to explain how to dial in, the questions became even more frenzied: "But, what happens if . . ." and "Explain to me how in the world . . . ," they stuttered.

I was supposed to explain it all and soothe their fears as well. The best I could do was gasp, wheeze, clear my throat, and stifle coughs. Lil, the office manager, had her own set of interminable questions, but peppered them with "Just take your time, Love." We remained secret comrades for years after that visit.

Several times during those six months, I sought help from doctors; dutifully, they prescribed stronger and stronger antihistamines. The drugs helped by completely drying out my nose and mouth and making me sleepy. Prescription drugs for such maladies were as primitive in 1984 as computers and modems.

There were many times when I wanted to light up—not to satisfy any urge but to ease the quitter's flu symptoms. Absurd, but smokers don't give absurdity any respect. After all, what's more absurd than taking a deep breath of carbon monoxide? Smokers even believe counter absurdities: "My grandmother smoked and lived to ninety-nine, when a bus ran her over." But the personal hygiene reason had taken root, along with the self-doubt reason to a lesser extent. I convinced myself that the annoying, disgusting symptoms of quitter's flu were a purge and that idea kept me going.

It was an emotional roller coaster. Some counselors recommend going off for a good cry during nicotine withdrawal, but I would excuse myself to run outdoors for a good cough and nose-blow. I had discovered new and indelicate body functions that belonged out of sight and earshot. I forced myself to cough until I brought up the prize—a brown-yellow chewy blob of phlegm—practically a biohazard. The coughing sounded like a snare drum and the nose-blowing like a kitchen sink that had suddenly unclogged. Both efforts left me exhausted and in a better mood—just like a good cry. I recommend doing this frequently—as often as you used to go outdoors for a cigarette.

There was unexpected encouragement along the way, too. I was physically cleaner and my sense of smell seemed twice as sensitive. I remember sitting alone in a classroom and, when the heat came on and stirred the air, getting a whiff of the Ivory soap I had used that morning. That happened about a month out—a tiny accomplishment I wanted to hoard and multiply. It was just like the time my mother showed me my bankbook after a year of saving dimes and quarters.

Acknowledge little signs of encouragement and your own quest will be much easier.

Speaking of money, I seemed to have more of it in my wallet. Today, when you give up seven-dollars-a-pack cigarettes, you can realistically expect to make a major investment with the newfound money. A car or down payment for a house is possible in a relatively short time. In 1984, an extra fifty cents a day in my pocket didn't buy much, but I noticed it nonetheless.

At the end of the six months, I buckled down and earned an A in both courses that semester, finally pushing my average safely above 3.0 and into solid B territory. I considered myself a scholar. So much for the self-doubt. Back at work, the modem/computer hookup was working well and had actually replaced a couple of old routines. I looked forward to talking with Lil. She still asked tiresome questions, but I could answer at length in a strong, confident voice.

After twenty years, I find myself in a related but unlikely career: technical writing for computers. I'm still explaining new technologies to unwilling users—mostly in writing but sometimes in person. Once in a while, especially if I strain my voice, the memory of those six months returns. But now I remember the accomplishments more than the quitter's flu.

SURVIVAL HINTS

1. Don't give in to self-doubt when you're trying to quit smoking.
2. Have a good cough and nose-blow to clear out the gunk. You'll be surprised what your body is trying to eject when you're detoxing from all that nicotine.
3. Add up all the money you've saved by not smoking! You'll be able to do something great with it.

2

When You're Using Hypnosis, Acupuncture, and Drugs to Quit

Sanity Quiz

The prescription product your doctor provided to curb
your smoking is affecting you in more ways than one.
In reading the fine print, you realize you are experiencing many adverse side effects, including fuzzy vision.

Do you
A. stick to the plan and deal with the weird effects
B. ask your doctor to provide you with a new
   prescription
C. appreciate the new look everything has and
   continue on
D. quit the plan and light up

No matter how you answered these questions, read
on and discover how these folks managed with various
different methods to quit smoking. And you think *you*
have problems?

You Are Getting
Very Sleepy

Angela Barton

MY GOOD FRIEND ERNIE AND I *really, really* wanted to quit smoking this time. I had signed us up for one of those Learning Annex courses; this one was with a hypnotist who specialized in "smoking cessation." A one-time shot, we would walk into the hotel conference room as smokers and emerge three hours later as nonsmokers. It sounded too good to be true, but also impossible to resist.

We headed to the seminar full of optimism. I pictured my carefree, healthy, nonsmoking self engaging in an astonishing variety of activities: blissfully running hand-in-hand with a lover on the beach, having cocktails with friends aboard a yacht, bicycling through France. Apparently, smoking had been the one thing holding me back from living a truly perfect life, one of beauty, ease, comfort, fun, and fabulous people.

These thoughts were interspersed in a kind of psychotic montage: scenes of fear, loss, and horror vaguely reminiscent of Edward Munch's painting *The Scream*. After all, if I gave up cigarettes, I would be saying good-bye to a very close friend. Like pets, cigarettes are there for you always, nonjudgmental and accepting. Come to think of it, they can be even more comforting and reliable than a pet. Because your cat sometimes acts as if she could take you or leave you, and your dog gives you looks that suggest he's thinking maybe he could have done better than you. Maybe someone who takes him out for a run once in a while. Maybe a nonsmoker.

About thirty people were packed into the small conference room. A corpulent middle-aged man who introduced himself as Bob put on a show in the front of the room. The performance reminded me of a circus act; I strongly suspected he came from that line of work. He used his arms, his legs, and even his head and neck as props as he animatedly flailed them around. The effect was that of a giant marionette.

There was also something of the religious zealot with his declaration that we would be "reborn." Ernie looked at me and raised one eyebrow.

Bob tried to convince us that hypnosis works. He cited statistics, related anecdotes, distributed handouts. Then he said the time had come to hypnotize us. That made me want a cigarette. It was only an hour into the event, and he did in fact offer us a break for what he referred to as "the last cigarette of our lives." I decided not to smoke after all, but Ernie couldn't wait to light up.

After the break, Big Top Bob told us to close our eyes and make ourselves comfortable. He didn't produce amulets for us to focus on. In a voice so nasal that he sounded in need of immediate oral surgery he droned on about relaxing every part of our bodies and breathing in the air around us. He intoned: "You have no need for cigarettes" and "You are a vital, healthy being."

I began to obsess about this guy's weight. After all, if he was such a great hypnotist, why didn't he hypnotize *himself* to cut back on the nachos? He must have weighed more than three hundred pounds. After we had endured about twenty minutes of a voice that was more irritating than relaxing, the man clapped his hands and told us to open our eyes. We were offered another break, and he said we could smoke if we wanted to. I thought that was sadistic. After all, he'd already called the previous break a chance to smoke "the last cigarette of our lives." I began to suspect that this guy was a charlatan.

But, strangely, I really didn't want a cigarette. Maybe it was working after all. Ernie went outside to smoke while I pondered my glamorous future as a nonsmoker, philanthropist, and newsmaker. After the second break, Bob passed out more handouts and talked a little bit about self-control and the power of the mind. Then, in a disappointingly low-key finale, he congratulated us and sent us off to begin our new lives.

On the way to the car, Ernie smoked a cigarette. I, on the other hand, was a nonsmoker. I truly didn't want to smoke. I believed something had happened to me in that room. Even though Ernie was smoking, he considered himself in the process of quitting, so we agreed to meet the next day to help each other through withdrawals. We decided to see a matinee movie.

We met at noon at the theater. I still hadn't smoked. Ernie had decided to give it a serious go and hadn't smoked at all that day. We saw a film called *Scandal*—presumably about a political scandal that had taken place in London in the 1960s and had involved a prominent politician and a call girl. There was lots of intrigue, beautiful people, and plenty of sexual situations. But it became immediately obvious that everyone in the film smoked constantly. In fact, the longer we watched, the more we realized that it was actually *about* smoking. The camera lingered on the manicured hands of the beautiful leading lady as the leading man lit her cigarette and stared into her eyes. The camera followed the cigarette to her lovely lips as she inhaled and smiled with satisfaction. These people clearly enjoyed smoking more than they enjoyed sex! At one point—and I'm not making this up—the screen was filled with a loving, even erotic, image of a lit cigarette falling through the frame in extreme close up. We bolted from the theater, tripping over each other as we went. We barely made it to the coffee house next door; but as soon as we got there, we inhaled our cancer sticks almost in a single drag. At that moment, becoming a nonsmoker seemed not only impossible but undesirable.

I successfully quit smoking for good later that year, almost thirteen years ago. But I did a lot of things differently. I did it on my own, not with someone I'd shared literally thousands of cigarettes with over the years. I told everyone I knew that I was quitting and I asked for their support. I sent away for all kinds of literature from the American Cancer Society. I wanted to see pictures of the horrible, gooey, tar-stained black lungs so that I would be motivated to save my own lungs from cancer. I also received lots of tips, strategies, and advice from the mailings, such as what to do when you want to smoke. The list included such things as going for a walk, taking a bath, and calling a friend. The basic idea is to distract yourself long enough to overcome the craving.

I also signed up for hypnosis, but this time I attended three private sessions. I still believed I had felt something during that Learning Annex seminar in spite of the presentation. It doesn't work for everyone, and it has to be a part of a total strategy, but hypnosis did help me.

Most of all, I had a strong feeling that enough was enough. I was thirty years old, I'd been smoking for more than a decade, and my grandfather had died of lung cancer before he was sixty. I really did want a new life for myself. So with the help of a professional hypnotist, good friends, and a lot of willpower, I gave up smoking for good.

And I really did get a new life. No yachts or trips to France—but love, work I enjoy, and lots of fun and laughs. I still miss cigarettes sometimes, but I like my new life a whole lot more.

SURVIVAL HINTS

1. Ask friends and family for support when you are trying to quit smoking—they all want you to succeed, and fewer people than ever want to be around smokers.
2. Scare yourself with whatever it takes to make you stop. Only you know what will really get to you, so be honest with yourself and go for it.
3. Distract yourself with other activities so that you don't think of smoking so much.
4. Try hypnosis—it really can work!

Wiggling the Staples: How I Quit Smoking with Acupuncture

Janice Kuta

IT ALL HAPPENED as kind of a lark. I am still amazed by how I quit smoking in the spring of 1989. From those trying to quit, I get a jaw-dropping expression, and from those who have already quit, a look of disbelief.

I called myself a "professional smoker," having smoked two and a half packs a day from the age of nineteen through the day that I unexpectedly and miraculously quit twenty-three years later. There were no immediate physical issues spurring me on, though

I kept hearing about how smoking was even more dangerous for women than for men. Smoking was still allowed in most restaurants and all public and private buildings and workplaces in New York City, but that would soon change.

It was my significant other, Jim, who brought this miracle about. Jim was longing to sail in the Indian Ocean with a friend who didn't allow smoking on his boat, so we had talked to two other sailors who had quit for similar reasons. Both had quit through acupuncture.

We got the name of an acupuncturist who practiced at his Park Avenue office. He turned out to be a nice young guy who had earned his medical degree in the Midwest. He had a thriving, what I called "bloodless" practice focusing on smoking, allergies, and weight loss. I recall that the cost of the acupuncture and six-week follow-up was $300 (sixteen years ago, remember!), and that was less than I paid for a suit. So, although Jim was committed to making this work (he smoked even more than I did), I thought that if it worked (with no real help from me) it would be great; if not, I would lose only a small investment.

We both smoked in the taxi all the way from Fifth Avenue and Sixteenth Street to Park Avenue. It is hard to believe that people were smoking in taxis back then! I remember crushing out our cigarettes on the street as we departed the taxi. We walked into a lovely waiting room and a few minutes later the young and handsome physician appeared.

With a surgical staple gun the doctor put one staple into the cartilage inside each of my ears. It didn't hurt much, and took only a second. He told me to keep my ears clean and wiggle the staples regularly and often; this would stimulate the energy center for nicotine addiction. He then scheduled weekly follow-up appointments to ensure that no infection had set in where the staple was set. The staple would fall out by itself in about six weeks. The doctor also dispensed bottles of vitamins, and that was that.

We left the office and went home. The round trip had taken about one hour. I couldn't ever remember not smoking for an entire hour unless I was sleeping. When we arrived home, I decided to go shopping (a normal activity for me) because one couldn't smoke in stores and shops. I went to the nearest Barnes & Noble and scouted around for books about quitting smoking.

I spent about an hour in the store and came away with *Quitting Smoking in 30 Days,* a tiny book published by the American Medical Association. I took the book home and realized I had gone two hours without smoking. I started wiggling my staples because I had thought about cigarettes. But I wasn't craving, I was just thinking.

The first pieces of advice I found in my new book was that I should practice deep breathing. It is a great tactic to relieve stress and helped with the fact that I missed inhaling. The book was designed to describe what would happen physically and psychologically each day during the first thirty days of quitting. I decided that each morning I would read that particular chapter only. By the eighth hour without a cigarette, I was still wiggling staples and watching television, but without cigarettes.

After about ten hours without a cigarette, I knew that something miraculous was happening, especially when the phone rang. I had always automatically reached for my cigarettes while I was talking on the telephone. This time, I went for the cigarettes, but then I said to myself, "Oh, I don't smoke anymore." That was the last time I ever reached for a cigarette when I picked up the phone. Wiggle, wiggle throughout the night.

Now, for twenty-three years, I had always smoked a cigarette right after brushing my teeth in the morning and then again while having my first cup of coffee. The next day after the staples: I brushed my teeth. I made the coffee. I reached for the cigarettes. I told myself, "Oh, I don't smoke anymore." Never again did I go for a cigarette when I drank a cup of coffee. From that point on, I started reading a chapter a day in the AMA book. I also experienced all of the physical symptoms of quitting, including peeing green because the nicotine was being filtered out of my system.

I could hardly believe it was twenty-four hours and I hadn't had a real craving for a cigarette. Lots of wiggling, breathing, and shopping went on for the next thirty days. I also developed the strange habit of walking behind people who were smoking so that I could breathe in their second-hand smoke. I eventually stopped that. It was quite embarrassing, really.

Sad to say, Jim never could completely give up cigarettes. He cut down a lot, but he never quit.

The AMA book gave wise advice about what could trigger smoking all over again. Immediately after I quit, for sixty days my life was filled with triggers: illnesses, financial reversals, transatlantic flying. Yes, you could still smoke on airplanes in those days. I took my first flight and thought I would die without a cigarette, but I made it through!

Despite surviving everything else, my problem turned out to be hubris. I was convinced that now I had quit, I would never again have to worry about smoking. Wrong.

I attended a large and lovely Thanksgiving party in Charlottesville, Virginia, given by my friend Jane. Jane, a nurse, had quit smoking two years before I had, and she had recently lost her mother to lung cancer. It was past midnight and we had all had enough to drink. Then, on the other side of the room, I spied Jane: She was lighting up a cigar! Well, I thought, if

she could do that, I could have a postprandial cigarette. But the instant I had that thought, I swear I saw
a little gnome-like presence of the devil sitting on
Jane's shoulder; he was smiling at me and agreeing
that I could afford to have just one cigarette.

I realized then that hubris was my devil. I said:
"Devil, be gone!"

Lest you think that this has all been a bed of roses, I
did gain about twenty pounds, weight I put on not
from snacking but from eating everything on my plate.
I used to eat half the portion on my plate and then
light up. Now, though, I continued eating. The food
didn't taste better; eating was just something to do.

I seriously advise anyone who quits smoking to
watch portions and limit snacks, and then to get those
endorphins moving through some kind of physical exercise. You may also want to try acupuncture.

SURVIVAL HINTS

1. Check out Internet sites dealing with acupuncture to
   find out what is involved. There is very little discomfort, and many people have achieved great results
   with little effort. Also visit the Web site for the
   National Institutes of Health:
   http://nccam.nih.gov/health/acupuncture/.

2. Acupuncture is now covered by most medical insurance plans, and many will cover the entire cost of smoking cessation treatment under their preventive medicine programs. Before starting treatment, it's best to call your carrier to find out if it's covered, and if you need to have your treatment pre-certified to ensure payment.

3. Many hospitals have complimentary medicine departments that include acupuncturists, and this is also a good place to look for one.

4. If you can't readily find a local acupuncturist, visit the Web site for the American College for Advancement in Medicine (ACAM), www.acam.org/dr_search/, or call the hotline referral number, 1-888-439-6891, to find a doctor in your area.

5. Check www.NaturalHealers.com for acupuncture schools; they can refer you to local practitioners.

6. Medical doctors are also climbing onto the acupuncture bandwagon. If you feel more confident using an M.D. for your treatments, the American Academy of Medical Acupuncturists, www.medicalacupuncture.org/, provides a link to a list of physicians certified in acupuncture.

7. Many chiropractors also are licensed acupuncturists.

My Trip to Oz with Zyban

Ed Stevens

I QUIT. Several times, as a matter of fact. The first several attempts were short and sweet. I would torture myself and those around me for a few days and then smoke like a fiend. I had done this more than fifteen times, never fully coming out from behind the pack. Then I decided to turn to my doctor for help. What the hell, nothing else was working. He recommended that I try Zyban. Everyone was swearing by it at the time, and I thought it sounded worth a shot. So I went to the pharmacy, picked up the prescription, and followed the instructions exactly. Day one went well. I didn't smoke and it was tolerable. I can do this, I thought.

Day two, however, was a different story. It introduced me into a whole new world. A world of colors and swirls, spots and waves. I was driving a big truck down the street when it first hit me. The road was waving and the trees were bending in every direction. The colors of the rainbow were floating in front of me. I felt like I was on some kind of wild ride through a fun house or virtual reality game. I felt like I was in Oz. Or maybe it was Woodstock all over again. I'm not sure, but I think if this stuff were packaged under its street name, it'd be labeled blotter acid. How it can be sold legally, packaged as Zyban, is way beyond me. Maybe a more appropriate name would be HighMan. Because high I was.

After the ill effects of my trip to Oz via Zyban had subsided, back off to the doctor I went. This time, "The Wiz" prescribed an inhaler. This is the way I eventually ended up being smoke-free. It worked, and with minimal side effects and no more trips to Oz or Woodstock. It took me three months of sucking on the little plastic nicotine machine, but it worked. It looked ridiculous, yet the inhaler produced the results, which was the whole point.

I still have the need to stick something in my mouth from time to time, just out of habit. But now, instead of making the cigarette companies richer, I'm helping pay for the new wing on the Wrigley's gum plant.

SURVIVAL HINTS

1. Whatever it takes to quit, do it. If your first attempt doesn't work, keep looking until you find a method that does.
2. Find a healthier vice. The more nicotine you put into your body, the longer and harder it will be to detox.
3. Try gum or other chewables to help with the oral fixation and keep you from reaching for a cigarette.

3

When You're
Coping with a Quitter

The Tic Tac Man
Joyce Romano

When Your Mother-in-Law Quits
P. J. Dempsey

Sanity Quiz

Your mother has been a smoker for as long as you can remember. You're scared for her health and general well-being. You have asked her time and time again to quit, but she doesn't.

Do you
A. tell her she's a fool and that she had better get with the program because, if she doesn't, you're not taking care of her if she gets sick
B. try to get her into a support group
C. take her car away so that she can't go to the store without you
D. let her smoke her brains out

No matter which answer you chose, you need to read on and find out how to cope when someone you associate with quits smoking, whether that person be a friend, a family member, or a colleague.

The Tic Tac Man

Joyce Romano

I HAD A BOYFRIEND a few years back whose name was Rizzo. I soon realized that Rizzo and I were not very compatible. He did, however, have his good points; or, I should say, he had one very good point. He displayed enormous sexual talents in both staying power and in frequency. Please forgive my shallowness here, but after my divorce I didn't date for a long time; consequently, I found Rizzo's talents a refreshing change of pace, a novelty of sorts.

Rizzo also had a lot of annoying habits that quickly set my teeth on edge, but his most annoying habit was his Tic Tac addiction. You see, Rizzo was trying to quit smoking. Every time he wanted a cigarette, he popped a Tic Tac instead. Yet this wasn't the entire problem. The really insufferable part was that he saved the empty plastic Tic Tac containers. He kept them in his car. He saved them in drawers. If you looked through his kitchen, every drawer was filled with empty Tic Tac containers. In his bathroom cabinets, hundreds of them lurked. Everywhere you looked: Tic Tac containers. If you needed an aspirin, you had to dig through six inches of clackety-clacking plastic Tic Tac containers; inevitably, half of them fell out of the drawer and bounced around on the tile floor. It drove me nuts.

Well, I heard that Rizzo did eventually quit smoking for good, but I wasn't around to see it because I couldn't take one more Tic Tac. Not even all the great sex was worth enduring the Tic Tac infestation.

Years later, a good friend and I were driving home from a movie when we began discussing amusing sex stories. I told him about Rizzo. He asked to what I attributed the boyfriend's stamina and talents. I told him I didn't know for sure, but suspected that it had something to do with Tic Tacs.

He immediately drove to the nearest convenience store and bought himself a stash!

SURVIVAL HINTS

1. Chewing gum and mints are effective substitutes when you crave a cigarette.
2. If you use mints to help quit smoking, throw away the empties if you want to keep your girlfriend.
3. Quitting smoking improves your sex life!

When Your Mother-in-Law Quits

P. J. Dempsey

TAKE IT FROM ME, quitting smoking yourself is a piece of cake compared to convincing an elderly relative to do the same. The example here is my eighty-eight-year-old mother-in-law, who has defied all the odds. Not only has she lived longer than the actuaries have predicted, but she's done it in spite of being a lifelong two-to-three-pack-a-day smoker.

She smoked her last Misty ultra light cigarette three months ago. If you ask her, she'll probably tell you the number of months, weeks, days, hours, and minutes since she took her last puff (which is exactly what it was because her reduced lung capacity made it impossible for her to inhale). No one ever thought she'd quit (including her), but it was a long, smelly, and nicotine-stained road to that unplanned last cigarette.

I remember when I first made the acquaintance of my future mother-in-law. At that time, more than twenty years ago, my widowed mother-in-law, Lee, lived with her younger sister, Nora, in the house she had once shared with her husband and four children. By then, she had outlived her husband by more than thirty years. He had died young when my husband was only four years old. Lee still talks about how her husband grudgingly bought her what he called her "coffin nails."

Glancing around the house, I noticed that there were multiple ashtrays in every room, and a few on the dining room table, too, which was the center of activity in the house. The walls throughout the apartment were a uniform shade of mustard yellow; my husband once told me that he never knew that lamp shades came in white. Lee and Nora carried their cigarettes and disposable lighters around with them, inside the house and out. Even when Nora quit (her health was failing), Lee didn't. When Nora passed away, the smoking escalated—I'm sure to while away the time and the loneliness. Even the cat started taking on the yellow tinge of the walls! That's when the family started voicing their concern about that and the wheezing—and the burned furniture.

The nonsmoking campaign started; actually, it went on for years. Everyone pointed out just how much Lee was smoking as we watched her light one cigarette off of another, while telling us how much she had cut down. She also developed the habit of not regularly tapping the ash into the ashtray, and there she'd be with what seemed like a two-inch-long ash dangling precariously from the end of a lit cigarette, which in turn dangled from the corner of her mouth as she spoke. I swore she was the model for the Hallmark card lady, Maxine (before they stopped drawing her with a cigarette).

When Lee came to visit, I made sure that the good tablecloths were put away because there would inevitably be a burn hole in the tablecloth within fifteen minutes of her arrival. She burned my husband's favorite chair and our living-room carpet, both on her first visit to our new house—a record. But where Lee went, the cigarettes followed, and the birthdays kept coming, even her big eightieth, where she was the only one at the party who still smoked.

The years went by, nonsmoking friends passed away, and even her doctor died. Her new doctor told her that if she quit she'd live to be a hundred. She informed him that she didn't care much about fulfilling that prophecy, so she'd just keep smoking.

Then came the conspiracy to stop the supply of cigarettes. The northeastern winters make the sidewalks treacherous for elderly ladies who walk with canes, and as Lee was growing frail she was unable to make the trek to the corner grocery for her "fix." We figured that would do it. Not so! Now she was getting them in the mail from her daughter who lived a few hundred miles away.

We had to hand it to her, she was creative, but she didn't hold a candle to our friend Pat's Aunt Agnes. Aunt Agnes lived on fried steaks, bourbon, and cigarettes. After her stroke, which affected her speech more than her capacity to get around, she had to be moved into a nursing home. Once there, deprived of her favorite vice, she was once found poking around in the parking lot looking for butts!

Lee was satisfied with her new nicotine connection, and she felt that all was right with the world. Then it became apparent that she would have to move from her beloved home. She was the sole resident in a huge house that was costing a fortune to keep up.

After the house was sold, Lee moved into a lovely new one-bedroom apartment. Everything was perfect—well, almost; you see, packages could not be delivered to the building. Tenants had to pick them up at the post office. There was no place to leave packages, and the mailboxes were too small for anything except envelopes and magazines. Now the mail connection was out of business, and the local relatives were not going to supply cigarettes. Yes, there was a store about two blocks away, but the smoking had taken its toll. That and not enough proper food was making Lee an unhealthy senior. Yet she still somehow managed to get her cigarettes (in addition to the ones we'd seen her bum from people when we took her out to dinner); we suspect that she somehow made it to that store.

She insisted she wasn't smoking, but the new white walls were starting to take on that familiar yellow look. Then she came down with pneumonia. Why that scared her straight, we don't know. She'd been hospitalized once before for six weeks without a cigarette; the first thing she did when she got back home was find her hidden stash and light one up (despite the fact that her granddaughter, a trained investigator with a degree in criminal justice, thought she'd found and tossed them all while Lee was in the hospital).

But today things are different. She hasn't smoked for a while. She's gained weight, she has more energy, her mind is sharper, and she's enjoying her new apartment. She has finally made the connection between health and not smoking. If she wants to live a healthy, independent life, she must remain—like the rest of us—a nonsmoker.

That's not to say that she's totally without vices. We are now "suppliers" to an eighty-eight-year-old chocoholic—and she doesn't want the cheap stuff.

4

When You Fall Off
the Butt Wagon

Feel the Burn
Edward F. Fitzgerald

I Couldn't Tap into the Magic
Peter Mastracchio

Sanity Quiz

You haven't smoked in more than four weeks and it's been pure hell. You get into an argument with a coworker, and the first thing you do is go into the bathroom and light up. Two cigarettes later, you are back at your desk feeling terrible and guilty.

Do you
A. throw in the towel and become a smoker again
B. promise yourself you will try harder next time and go have a smoke
C. tell your coworker what a jerk he is and that it's his fault you smoke

If you answered yes to any of these questions, you need to read on. Most people quit several times before it sticks, and here are some of their stories.

Feel the Burn

Edward F. Fitzgerald

GEORGE DEMOLAY SAT at his kitchen table pawing his morning mail and picking up and throwing circulars in the direction of the wastebasket. A cigarette dangled from his lower lip. He'd acquired the trick of wetting it and sticking it to his lip so that he could open his mouth and drink coffee without removing the butt.

George's wife, Marian, also known as Pittypat, also referred to by George as My Significant Owner, was standing over the toaster, watching it with one eye. The other eye was closed because of the smoke curling up toward her face from the twisted black cheroot cigar she held pointed at the ceiling between the first two fingers of her left hand.

When the handle of the toaster abruptly popped, Marian jumped; one slipper flew off and sailed into the corner, where one of their five cats caught it before it landed. Making "prey" noises, the cat ran from the room, clutching the slipper in its jaws, to let the others know it had nailed something gamey. "The cats are smarter'n you are," George muttered. "Every morning you jump, every morning Maxwell catches. He gets through chewing and slobbering on it, that slipper looks like a possum, been dead for a week."

Marian walked toward the table tossing the piece of toast up and down in one hand to keep it from burning her, until she missed. Then the toast bounced once on the table and landed on top of the letter George had just flattened in front of him. He picked up the toast without comment and took a bite. "Owtch! That's hot!" he muttered.

George pointed at the letter with the extended baby finger of his eating hand. "They think they're getting fifty back from me, they are crazier than I thought," he offered, taking a second and larger bite.

"Who?" Marian queried. "What fifty? What are you talking about?"

"Those anal-retentive 'Staying Sane' idiots," George growled. "The ones running that 'Staying Sane While Quitting Smoking' program I told you about."

"You never told me they *paid* you to take part. You said it was a public service you were performing. And you flunked out anyway, didn't you?"

George sounded exasperated. "I did not *flunk* out of anything, Pittypat," he retorted. "I resigned. I declined further participation. I simply did not agree with the rigid parameters they insisted upon."

"Parameters? What parameters? You were supposed to quit smoking. Period. End of story. Right?"

"Yes. Those parameters."

"George," Marian said, taking a large puff from the ugly tube and sending another black plume floating toward the ceiling, "I *told* you not to sign up for that. You know you have the backbone of a jellied eel."

"Rot!" George exploded. "A foul lie. I have plenty of backbone. Starts up here and runs right down to my . . . wallet pocket. And I can quit smoking anytime I want—anytime!"

"Sure you can, Pet. And you can start right up again, too, anytime. What does the letter say anyway? Looks like three or four pages."

"Never mind," George started to say, but Marian's hand shot out and snapped the pages away from him.

She backed across the room smoothing them as she began to read.

"Do *not* read that," George ordered. "It's all lies."

Pittypat's lips began moving as she read, but then she stopped, a wicked smile lighting her features. "They sent you a transcript of your interview, George. How nice."

Marian began to read the enclosure out loud. *"Interview conducted in the corporate offices of Staying Sane Publications . . . "*

"Corporate offices!" George snorted, interrupting. "Second floor above a drugstore. Room was so small you had to step outside to change your mind. The hooks where the mops and brooms used to hang were still on one wall. They used kindergarten chairs to make the place look bigger."

"The interviewee is George Demolay, one of the partici-pants in the 'How to Stay Sane While Quitting Smoking' program. The interviewer is a professional journalist hired by the corporation . . . "

"Professional journalist!" George choked on a gulp of smoke and coughed loudly. "Prissy little kumquat. Smacked his lips the whole time like a starving man reading a menu."

"Shut up, George," Marian said. She sat down in the chair next to the window and began to read the transcript out loud. She asked the questions in a bright, inviting tone, and then read George's answers in a cranky, growling undertone.

Q. Ah, Mr. Demolay. How nice you could make it this morning. Please, have a seat. Coffee? Oh, I see you have brought your own. Interesting. I didn't know Starbucks had half-gallon containers.

A. I've been drinking more coffee since.

Q. Since?

A. Since I quit smoking.

Q. Oh, quite understandable. Quite, I assure you. Now, let's see Mr., uh—

A. George. You may call me George.

Q. Uh, George. Fine. Now this is Monday morning, about nine, and you have now been off the tobacco habit as we call it, since . . . just how long is it?

A. *[Looking at his watch.]* Roughly, oh, say, forty-five minutes.

Q. But I was told you quit weeks ago.

A. I did.

Q. Ah, wait. I see. You quit but then you started back up again?

A. Right. Three weeks ago last Friday.

Q. Alright, I understand. Now, that first time when

you quit, on that Friday, how long was it before you started smoking again?

A. A good hour, I'd say. Maybe a bit more. Call it sixty-five minutes.

[A longish silence. The sound of what might have been lips pursing can be heard on the tape.]

Q. And, uh, then you started smoking again?

A. Like a chimney. The quitting, you know? It was like a spur in the rump when I started up again. The deprivation and all.

Q. The deprivation? You mean the sixty-five minutes? I see. And since then, did you try again?

A. Oh, yes. Twice. The next Monday, and again this past Monday. Determined I was, really. Once I get the bit in my teeth to do something, I'm a dog. My wife will tell you that. Little Caesar, she calls me, after a Pomeranian we had once. Choked on a chew toy, wouldn't let go of it. Buried him with it still in its little jaws—

Q. *Mister* Demolay. George. May we continue? Please. Those two later attempts. They lasted how long?

A. Well, not as long as that first try.

Q. You mean, *less* than an hour? Two attempts, less than an hour each?

A. Put that way, I grant you, it may not seem like much, but it was hell. Pure hell.

Q. You don't think—isn't it fair to call your participation a total failure?

A. A *total* failure? Certainly not. A less than stellar success, I'll give you that. But not a *total* failure. I won't have that.

Q. In what way, may I ask, would you say that your participation was not a total failure?

A. Well, I gave them up, didn't I? Turned my back on them. Gave them the big fat "N-O," didn't I? Not once, not twice, but *three* times, not counting this morning. With my deprived heart pounding away, with every nerve and fiber of my being crying out for a ciggie. With my—

Q. Yes, yes, yes. But for how *long*, Mr. Demolay? For how *long*?

A. Minutes, yes. We agreed on that. But long, endless, excruciating minutes, let me tell you, and—

Q. *Under an hour?* Less than one bloody hour, and you call that quitting? I was a three-pack-a-day man and I quit smoking, quit cold. I haven't touched one to this day since the Red Sox won the World Series.

A. In *1908?* You *are* very well preserved, I must say—

Q. Not 1908, you fool. *Last* year, in 2004.

A. Here now, no need to shout at me. You're getting very red in the face. Can't be good for a man of your advanced years. Even if you were a child in 1908, you must be at least—

Q. *Mister* Demolay. Enough. I think we've finished our business here. You took our fifty dollars and never made even a half-hearted attempt to quit, and you know it.

[Sound of a scratching noise.]

Q. Mr. Demolay! Stop! You *can't* smoke here in our offices!

A. Well, it's your fault. You've made me nervous. I always smoke when I'm nervous.

Q. Get out. Get out of this office. *Now!*

A. Well, but you've forgotten something, haven't you? Understandable for an old timer like you, I suppose, but still. You haven't validated my parking ticket.

[Sounds of men grappling, a chair toppling, a door slamming. Interview terminated.]

Marian Demolay was wiping tears from her eyes and making noises like a cat who had successfully upped a hair ball onto a newly ironed dress. George, lighting another cigarette from the last bit of the old one, felt rather miffed. "I called a lawyer," he said. "You know the one. That witch who burned those two city councilors last year for not having open meetings.

Told her Staying Sane owed me $2.50 for parking *and* the tenner they promised for the interview. Told her I wanted to sue their rumps off."

Marian, still gasping and holding her sides, could barely speak: "What'd she say?" she gasped.

"Said she'd have to check and see when the World Court was next sitting at The Hague. Said there was no sense going local with a case that size. Smart-ass shyster."

George re-read the letter and, as he did so, he ground out his current coffin nail with an unusual firmness, twisting it into the flank of the Budweiser horse on their kitchen ashtray. "You know what hurts?" he asked, a note of pensiveness in his voice that surprised Marian, "the idea that they thought I really didn't try. That I wasn't serious. That I had no intention of quitting when I took their lousy thirty pieces of silver."

"Fifty," she corrected.

"Whatever. Well, you know what? I'm going to show them what George Pierpont Demolay can do when he gets his Irish up. What do you think of that?"

"George, your middle name is Wilbur."

"Never mind. I like the rich ring of Pierpont, and I can change it if I want. Here," he told her, sliding the small pack with the cowboy on it across the kitchen table, "discard these, my love. The evil weed has run its course with George Pierpont Demolay!"

Marian shook the box next to her ear like a cheap watch. "Empty," she announced, and then scaled it into the wastebasket with a softball sidearm. George hated it when she did that. She never missed.

"How about this *carton*, Pierpont," she asked, and like a kimonoed conjurer, she brought his last stash out of the table drawer. "Shall I give it a perfidious fate, too?"

George gulped and swallowed hard, but then sat up straighter and nodded. The long rectangle hit the basket with a crash and toppled in. George didn't even whimper. Marian was impressed. "Okay, Handsome," she said, pulling the package of cheroots from her kimono pocket and flinging them after the cigarettes, "two can play this game. I'm with you. First one to waver is a sucking swamp toad."

"Deal," said George Pierpont Demolay, rising to his full five feet and seven inches and extending a hand to his grinning wife. "In no time we'll be flush with re-newed youth and vigor. By God, I'm going to buy a skateboard!"

There is no question about it. It was just the one eye. One of the watching cats winked.

SURVIVAL HINTS

1. If you fail to quit smoking, don't be surprised. But remember that every day you don't smoke is a bonus for your lungs, not to mention the people around you, so even if you start up again for a while, you're still ahead.
2. Don't give up, even if you fall off the butt wagon. Every day is a fresh start, and that applies to quitting smoking, too.
3. Don't beat yourself up if you end up smoking again. Just climb right back up on the butt wagon and take care of yourself!

I Couldn't Tap into the Magic

Peter Mastracchio

A FEW DAYS AFTER the hypnosis class, nicotine withdrawal got the better of me and I lit up. Disappointment is an old friend to all smokers who try to quit, but this caused a pernicious self-doubting of my abilities and strengths. I wondered whether I could ever do anything right—or if I had ever done anything right until then.

Hypnosis had seemed like magic. Nobody needed to hype it. What could be more powerful than my own mind? What could be more convenient? It made so much sense that it had to be foolproof. I arrogantly considered the next conquests after smoking, settling vaguely on wealth and romance.

The three-hour class was held in a modest local hotel, the chairs and tables arranged classroom style. The instructor was intentionally nondescript in his gray suit and solid tie. His mannerisms were professional and rehearsed. His voice was clear and unequivocal, devoid of any inflection that would seem commanding or dramatic.

The first exercise began. Each one of us held a small lead weight clipped onto a nylon string six inches above a card. A vortex was printed on the eight-inch-square card. The lights dimmed and we were instructed to swirl the lead weight gently over the vortex and let our minds go blank. The pea-sized lead weight and thin nylon monofilament immediately recalled happy childhood memories of fishing for snapper off City Island.

The vortex reminded me of the opening sequence of *The Twilight Zone*. I could almost hear the first few bars of that unmistakable eerie music and Rod Serling's familiar intonations. The engine of hypnosis is to first make your mind a blank canvas and then paint it with vivid suggestions. Like most hypnosis first-timers, I was bumping into the first hurdle. It's not so easy to quiet the mind. Sneaky thoughts were behaving like willful two-year-olds refusing to go to bed.

We were told to feel our major muscle groups relax, one by one—and, above all, to refrain from thinking about anything. I was surprised by how difficult it was to stop thinking and relax my muscles at the same time. The reward for getting it right was a contented feeling, almost like drifting off to sleep with a full stomach. A gentle warning came from the instructor that we might feel tingling or a sensation of warmth or cold. This phenomenon is actually reported often by people undergoing hypnosis. It manifested in me as intermittent itching around my knees and ankles, which only added to the mystique and believability of hypnosis. Thankfully, those were the only body parts affected.

Next, we were told to imagine using both hands to hold a large, overflowing ashtray an inch beneath our noses. There was an abrupt transition from the sublime to the disgusting. The instructor's tone did not change from his earlier soothing invitations to relax. The obvious intent was to burn a vivid image into an idle, suggestible mind. It worked so well that, even after twenty-five years, I can remember every detail. The hardest of hardcore smokers would wretch at the sight and smell of gray ashes and mangled crushed-out butts. Muffled grunts and moans arose one by one from my classmates as the image became more vivid.

We received a second image to drive the point home. The overflowing ashtray had almost been enough to make me gag. It was as if a crazed roller coaster operator had given his terrified riders an unwanted second ride for free.

Next we were invited to picture the familiar routine and all the details of waking up in the morning, lighting up, and taking that satisfying first drag. We were further asked to smoke that cigarette all the way down to the end, and then light the next one from it—and to repeat those steps until all twenty cigarettes in the pack were gone. After two or three of these mental cigarettes, my nausea became real. That experience alone convinced me that thoughts are real things.

Hypnosis is a credible science. Hypnotherapy, its application to diseases and conditions, is a valid medical procedure according to no less an authority than the American Medical Association. The University of Maryland Medical Center's Web site lists many ailments that have been successfully treated by hypnotherapy. They mostly seem to involve chronic pain and/or anxiety.

When it comes to smoking (and other addictions), hypnotherapy's success cannot be measured so easily. By some estimates, as much as 25 percent of the general population is unhypnotizable, and these individuals are probably not screened out of stopsmoking hypnosis classes. More important, no study measures how much any one technique contributes to eventual success. It's probably safe to say that almost nobody in the history of smoking has ever quit by using one technique on a single occasion.

Hypnosis didn't work for me—at least, not immediately. As real as the images and physical revulsion had been, I didn't give up cigarettes for good until four years later. During those years, I attempted to quit by trying other techniques—including cold turkey and more group support meetings than I can count. But when they failed, smoking again never felt as bad as that first cigarette a week after hypnosis class.

More than the vivid image of the overflowing ashtray and the nausea, I remember being disgusted with myself for not tapping into the promised magic of hypnosis. That was in 1979, and it seemed that the rest of the world had discovered and was using the creative powers of the mind. Mike Love of the Beach Boys embraced Transcendental Meditation. John Lennon and Yoko Ono published "A Love Letter from John and Yoko" in the *New York Times*. It began: "The past ten years we noticed everything we wished came true in its own time, good or bad, one way or the other." My failure to quit through hypnosis couldn't be any more uncool and inept; it was akin to never being chosen for the good team in the schoolyard.

I never lost my enchantment with creative visualization; in fact, it served me in other aspects of my life, long after my last cigarette. I still re-read my well-worn books by Wayne Dyer, Shakti Gawain, Jose Silva, and a few others. I even have the venerable Norman Vincent Peale's *Positive Imaging* and James Allen's *As a Man Thinketh.*

Although I'm not an expert, I was and still am truly infatuated with the idea that thought can become reality—or conquer an addiction such as smoking. All these erudite authors were saying so, along with Mike Love and John and Yoko. I don't know whether any of them would appreciate being connected to a one-night quit-smoking session in a hotel ballroom, but for me they are.

I once proved to myself that their principles work. I was stuck in a miserable job and had somehow set up an interview for a dream job at a dream company. All weekend before the interview, I immersed myself in material about the company. I pictured myself in working there alongside the glamorous people shown in the company's brochures. I got the job, and the people in the photos turned out to be real employees. I worked with them all during the years I spent there.

Of course, I didn't realize at the time that my depressing failure to quit smoking through hypnosis would become a building block for my eventual success. Maybe positive imaging (like my dream job) would have worked better than the negative imaging of the hypnosis class. There are scientific opinions on both sides of that question. Although it was so painful at the time, I don't regret my failure. It was a catalyst.

Why not look at your own failed quitting attempts in the same way? After a big-time loss in the stock market, you can either quit or get serious with your research and financial discipline. That's a relatively easy lesson because only money is involved, not your abilities and strengths.

The hypnosis session didn't cost much, but I knew it was money down the drain. Because it was only a few hours—slightly longer than a bad movie—I couldn't complain about wasted time.

That failure to tap into the magic of hypnosis—so mysterious, so filled with promise, so seemingly foolproof—was a huge letdown and I viewed it as a personal failure. But rather than let smoking win, I determined that the next time, or the time after that, I'd find a way, a technique, or a method to help me make it, until I finally did.

If I have any advice to offer, it's this: Just don't give up—keep trying until you finally quit. I did it and you can, too.

SURVIVAL HINTS

1. You may need to try more than one technique to quit smoking for good. Don't be afraid to explore more than one option.
2. Many people don't succeed the first time they quit, so keep at it for as many attempts as you must to get free of your smoking addiction.
3. Hypnosis, aversion therapy, and visualization work well for many people, and they can also be applied to other aspects of your life as an added bonus once you learn them.

5

When You Go to Extremes to Quit

Sanity Quiz

You are marooned on a desert island. You have a pack of cigarettes but only one match. You are freezing to death and want to start a fire to keep warm. But you know deep down that you don't have enough lit-match time to light up a smoke and get the fire ignited at the same time.

Do you
A. light the smoke and say to hell with all else
B. freeze to death but happily because you have had one last smoke
C. don't do either; instead, save your last match until you're rescued and then have a celebratory smoke
D. light the fire first and then light your smokes from it

If you answered yes to any of these questions, you need to read on and find out how this batch of ex-smokers quit while under extreme duress!

Sparks Were Flying

Joyce Romano

WHEN I WAS JUST A KID, my brothers and I would visit our Uncle John on his farm out in the country. It was an old-fashioned farm, complete with pig pens and an outhouse. We loved to pet the animals, milk the cows, and help Uncle John pull corn. But one of my fondest memories is of the Fourth of July in 1957; that's when the sparks really flew.

Every summer we would spend Independence Day at the farm. Uncle John would buy a big bag of fire-crackers to set off and thrill us. We were getting to the age where we wanted to set them off ourselves, but to keep us from being hurt, Uncle John would pass out only one firecracker at a time and make sure we lit it correctly.

On this particular Fourth of July, after we had set off a few firecrackers, Uncle John had to "go see a man about a horse" and started off for the outhouse. But knowing my brothers and I would get into trouble while he was gone, he grabbed the bag of firecrackers and took them with him into the outhouse.

Moments later, we saw him burst out of the outhouse in a run and trip over his pants—which were around his ankles. He fell just outside the door. He was screaming at all of us to run away as he tried to recover and get away himself.

Within a few moments, the outhouse erupted in a cacophony of whistles and explosions as all the firecrackers and roman candles went off at the same time, throwing sparks and fireworks all over the place and sending everyone running in every direction.

We later found out that while he was sitting on the throne, he decided to have a smoke. He lit a match, put it to his cigarette, and then, without thinking, he dropped the lit match directly into the paper bag of firecrackers. Within seconds he realized what he had done, but it was too late because the bag had already caught on fire. The only thing Uncle John had time to do was open the door and attempt to run . . . with his pants still down around his ankles.

Needless to say, Uncle John was in a messy situation. Once clear of the immediate danger, we dropped to the ground in tears from laughing so hard as we watched him run towards the house to clean himself up.

That ended our fun for that day, but we all learned a valuable lesson. Never smoke on the throne with firecrackers nearby.

SURVIVAL HINTS

1. Cigarettes and firecrackers do not mix.
2. It's an effective idea to dramatize for children the dangers of smoking.
3. Outhouses cannot withstand fireworks.
4. Try to quit before you, too, go up in smoke!

Rattlesnake Skins and Antifreeze

Ted Weaver

I WILL NOT PAY THIS MUCH for a pack of cigarettes! Highway robbery! Criminal! Must be a conspiracy! Just think, for the same money, I could buy a gallon of gas and two sodas! Time to quit.

A news article had the answer: Discipline. Good old all-American self-discipline. Decided to do it and then just did it! Tremendous mental focus, and no cigarettes for . . . seven minutes and thirty seconds! Maybe tomorrow. Yes! And a new record: Eight minutes! Self-discipline takes too much discipline. Must be an easier way.

Why quit smoking? Burned a hole in the lap of my best suit pants while driving. Could have been serious. Need to quit now.

Someone knew someone somewhere who was rumored to have kicked the habit by chewing gum instead of lighting up. The world contains 356 varieties of gum. I know because I tried them all—everything from bubble gum to breath sweetener. Spent just a little less than the monthly smoke tab, gained four pounds, and did the impossible: I chewed gum and smoked at the same time. Must be an easier way.

So why quit smoking! Yellow teeth! Really ugly, and the yellow comes from the chemicals in the cigarettes. Kinda clashes with my blue blood, red nose, and sexy brown eyes. Red nose in between yellow teeth and brown eyes looks like Bozo. Need to quit now.

Gum! How could I miss the obvious answer: Nicorette! Late night television ads gave me the idea. Cash paid, foul-tasting stuff chewed. I did not stop smoking, but I did stop watching late night television. Must be an easier way.

So why quit smoking? Bad breath. Just think of a fertilizer truck spilling its load on a road-kill skunk near a pulpwood plant—pleasant odors compared to a smoker's breath. Kisses are scarce and friends are, too. Need to quit now.

Patches and hypnotism worked about as well as the gum and discipline; in other words, not at all. The patches cost money. My hypnotist was also a pickpocket. He cost me money—and he stole my cigarettes! Bought myself some more. Need to quit now.

Finally found the real answer. Rattlesnake skins and antifreeze. Worked so well for me that I have been smoke-free for thirty-five years. Saved $25,550, a figure based on the low price of only $1 a pack, twice a day, for thirty-five years. All because of the rattlesnake skins and antifreeze.

My cigarette habit and I were invited to work in the skinning pit of the World's Largest Rattlesnake Roundup in Sweetwater, Texas. Hundreds of skins were to be made ready for the tourists who would attend the event. The skins were placed in large garbage cans full of antifreeze. The liquid was used to preserve the skins and stifle the odor until they could be sold to the tourists.

When you put your hands in antifreeze, you absorb glycol through your skin. If you hold a cigarette in your wet hand and smoke, you also inhale the glycol, which results in badly burned lungs. Lungs burned so badly that just breathing is torture. I could not even think of smoking a cigarette for several days, then several weeks, with badly burned lungs.

That's how I quit smoking easily, the hard way, and it worked! Skip the discipline, gum, patches, and hypnotism. Go for something that works: rattlesnake skins, antifreeze, and a cigarette!

Disclaimer: Neither the authors nor the publisher recommend trying this technique. Stick to accepted methods that are proven to be safe.

Quitting the Wrong Way

Jimmy Allen

THE FRESHMAN CLASS at college in the late 1980s was full of new smokers, and I was one of them. I never thought I'd be a smoker because I was a high school athlete who won regional wrestling competitions and enjoying star-status as a cross-country runner. But here I was, a healthy eighteen-year-old turned hard-core smoker of Marlboro Reds.

Like most other young smokers, I was excited about smoking. It made me feel older, more mature, and cool. I was so into it that I held a cigarette in my mouth when I walked to class; I would drag on the Marlboro and almost finish it without touching it with my hand.

Looking back, I am amazed. I could flick the ash with a quick move of my teeth. Looking back, I see how disgusting it was! I must have looked like a young fool.

As the year went on, I was smoking more than two packs a day. Fortunately, back then, cigarettes were fairly cheap, about $1.25 a pack, which was about the same price as a beer, and I drank a lot of them, too. As a broke college kid, I quickly realized that two packs a day added up, and I often found myself scrounging for change to buy more. I always had enough money for cigarettes, though.

Long drags on two packs a day do amazing things to young, pink, athletic lungs. After about six months of intense smoking, I began hocking up dark, sometimes black, and unusually sticky phlegm. One cool day as I was walking home from class with my trademark no-hands smoking and walking trick, I coughed a deep blob up into my throat. It made me immediately nauseous, and I spat it out onto the sidewalk. It looked like a small part of my lung, because it was hard, spongy, and sticky, and it immediately became cemented onto the surface of the sidewalk. The blob was as black as tar. I was scared to death.

When I arrived back at my dorm, my roommate Ben was there. As my best friend and roommate, he naturally didn't mind my smoking because we had started smoking together with the same Marlboro

Reds. I told him about my experience walking from class and how concerned I was. We talked about it for a while, and I announced to him that I was going to quit smoking once and for all. It was an abrupt decision, and a decision that, looking back, could have killed me.

There was a carton of Reds on a shelf, and I took out a box and started packing it by whacking the end of the pack to settle the tobacco. I decided that I was going to make myself sick on cigarettes, so sick that I'd never want another one for the rest of my life. I pitched my first idea to Ben: I would eat the pack of cigarettes, including the filter. Surely that would make me sick. Ben suggested instead that I smoke the entire box of cigarettes, one after the other, with heavy and long drags, and smoke them all down to the filter. That made a lot more sense to me than eating them.

I sat on the bed and Ben sat nearby on a desk chair. I arranged twenty Marlboros side by side on a towel. I lit the first one and smoked it faster than I had ever before smoked a cigarette, and even as a two-pack-a-dayer, I wanted to gag. The second one burned so hot that it hurt my lips a little and made my nose run. Then the third, the fourth, and the fifth. I took a breather for a few seconds, but Ben was shouting, "Keep going, keep going! Don't stop now or you'll ruin the experiment!" On I smoked.

The break helped because the sixth cigarette was not as hot and intense, perhaps because my pattern had been broken. It didn't take long to get it back. The seventh, eighth, and ninth went down in less than two minutes. My lungs were burning with hot cigarette poison and I could feel the junk coating my bronchial tubes. But I kept going.

Just a few minutes later, probably on number twelve or thirteen, Ben was hysterical with laugher because the air in our little dorm room was so thick with smoke. He grabbed the towel (I rescued the cigs with my left hand) and fanned the smoke out the window because he was worried that we would set off the smoke detector. Looking back, he should have been concerned about me!

Number seventeen. I could barely put it on my lips to light it because of the tremors. I was shaking like a naked man in the snow. My eyes were slits, irritated from all the smoke and the overdose of nicotine. I kept going. There were only three left. Eighteen. Nineteen. Ben was now shouting and laughing: "Only one more to go, you can do it, Jimmy!" I didn't know whether I could, or even if I should. I was very sick.

Twenty. It was the last cigarette of this smoking marathon, and hopefully the rest of my life. My stomach was churning as if I had drunk sour milk. My eyes were blood red, my eyelids were heavy, and my nose hairs were burnt. Ben was chanting and cheering me on: "Go, go, go, go!" I was dragging as hard on number twenty as I had on number one. Half the cigarette was now consumed; half to go.

During the next drag, my body erupted. I vomited bile from the depths of my liver. I threw up all over everything—the bed, my books, the floor, the television. It spewed. I tried to get up and find the bathroom, but I fell to the floor in agony instead. Couldn't breathe. Couldn't see. Ben was hysterical with laughter.

I knew that I had to get out of that smoky dorm room. I knew I needed a shower, but I didn't want to smell the smoke and mix it with water. I didn't want to smell my clothes. I wanted out of there, but I couldn't move.

After thirty minutes or so, Ben realized that I was seriously ill. He got me up, put my arm around his shoulder, and took me to a hotel. We both stayed the night, as far away from the smoky room as possible. Ben should have driven me straight to a hospital. Doctor friends today tell me that I could have easily died on the spot from cardiac arrest or nicotine overdose. How stupid we were. How stupid I was to even begin smoking.

This was the wrong way to quit, but it's the way I did it. From that day on, I was a nonsmoker, which is amazing because I had been a hard-core two-packer just minutes before. I never experienced nicotine withdrawal symptoms because it made me sick just to think about the fleshy, nasty stench of burned nose hair, the taste of vomit, and the sight of part of my black lung on the sidewalk.

I don't recommend quitting the way I did. It was stupid and I could have died that day. But the wrong and dangerous way worked for me. I could never, ever, under any circumstance or threat, smoke a cigarette again.

SURVIVAL HINTS

1. Never, ever, attempt to quit by oversmoking. There can be immediate and very serious health consequences.
2. There is such a thing as nicotine poisoning, just like alcohol poisoning, and it's irresponsible to encourage someone to overindulge with any substance or drug.
3. If someone you know overdoes it, it's best to call for immediate help rather than wait until it's too late. Better to be safe than sorry.

Disclaimer: Neither the authors nor the publisher recommend trying this technique. Stick to accepted methods that are proven to be safe.

6

When You're Scared into Quitting

Sanity Quiz

You've just read the latest warnings about smoking, and all the symptoms they've listed under irreversible damage match all of your symptoms.

Do you

A. go into shock and light up a butt
B. figure you're too far along in the disease to quit now, and so you keep smoking
C. call your doctor and tell him you think you're dying

If you answered yes to any of the questions or fall into any of these categories, then you're in the same boat as our contributors. Read on and find out how they managed under some harrowing fears and circumstances.

My Bet with Bernie

Lolly Paul

W AS I ADDICTED to cigarettes? In spades. Listen.

In the good old days, when I was pregnant, I was able to sit and smoke with a weighted beanbag ashtray on top of my big stomach. When I gave birth to twin girls, I breast-fed them, still smoking, trying not to drop ashes on them. At one point, I thought I saw too much smoke coming up and thought I had set their hair on fire.

They cried when I was breast-feeding them, and then one day they stopped. I think they were becoming addicted to ashes. When I told my doctor about this, he said it wasn't good for the babies. I had to do something drastic. So what could I do? I gave up breast-feeding. It was easier to juggle two babies, two bottles, and one cigarette.

My husband was a nonsmoker, and I thought that was about the only thing wrong with him. We used to spend a few weeks every winter in Palm Springs, California, and every New Year's Eve we went to a big house party thrown by some friends, Bill and Edna Bock. These were the days when smoking had become socially unacceptable, so when I wanted to smoke, I had to go outside to the Bock's back patio.

It was at that party where I met Bernie Maas, another confirmed smoker. Bernie was tall, slim, and strikingly good looking with sparkling blue eyes and golf-bronzed skin. That first New Year's Eve on the back patio, we got to know each other a bit, and we marveled that although we had both come to the Bock's New Year's party for years, we had never met.

At that first meeting, I learned that Bernie had started smoking when he was a Boy Scout; he called it his Smoking Merit Badge. I remembered that when I was eleven, I had a cigarette hanging out of my mouth while I was painting my first dollhouse.

We admitted to each other that we both wanted to quit smoking, and we made a pact that we'd meet every future New Year's Eve on the Bock's back patio and give each other a progress report. Then we made a ten-dollar bet, the winner to be the one who quit smoking first.

On every New Year's Eve thereafter, we touched upon just about every aspect of our smoking habits: the stigma that dictated lying to everybody, especially to loved ones, to the extent of taking "solemn oaths," dousing ourselves with strong-smelling mouth sprays and lozenges, and hiding in bathrooms and alleys (Bernie admitted that he once even inadvertently set fire to the toilet paper in a friend's bathroom, and the fire department showed up!).

On the other hand, we never lost sight of the unique pleasures of smoking as we conversed. For instance, it was wonderful to be able to smoke while having a relaxed chat on the telephone with a friend; it was just as wonderful to be able to smoke while screaming on the phone at a tradesman or a lawyer, or at my children.

I tried a long, Jean Harlow–type cigarette holder for a while, until I almost put somebody's eye out. I went through a period when I loved carrying one of those big boxes of wooden matches around and lighting up with them to get that tart smell of sulfur; but I quit doing that when I began to suspect that I was getting addicted to matches. I also enjoyed, believe it or not, smoking with a dab of Vick's Vaporub under my nose.

Over the years, when Bernie and I met, our main topic of conversation was essentially our attempts to stop smoking. One year we both tried filtered cigarettes, and we found ourselves tearing off the filters, turning the cigarette around, and enjoying the real thing. I confessed that I had failed to quit after attending the Schick Stop Smoking Clinic, not once, but twice; I admitted that I actually grew to love the smell of their dirty ashtrays! Bernie was one up on me: he failed three times at Schick and gave up the class when he saw one of the teachers sneaking a guess what in the alley.

I almost quit when my husband told me that his first wife had just given up smoking. I wasn't going to let her get one up on me! The only trouble was, she quickly fell off the wagon, and so did I.

I started chewing Nicorette, the cigarette-substitute gum, and I thought I was going to beat the habit and win my bet with Bernie! I was going to become a new woman. I got myself a complete face-lift and continued with the Nicorette. My face was perfect for a week or two, and then it began to fall apart. The surgeon explained that the constant chewing was destroying all his good work, and if I kept it up, I'd look like my old self again, or worse! Heaven forbid! I stopped chewing Nicorette and went back to smoking.

By the next New Year's Eve, I had practically given up trying. I waited for Bernie on the Bock's back patio, as always.

It got later and later, but he didn't show up. Finally, I went to Edna Bock to find out whether Bernie had called. She said, "Oh, I'm so very sorry to tell you. I thought you knew. Bernie died in the summer. Of emphysema."

That night I quit smoking. And unfortunately Bernie won the bet—after all, he did quit smoking first.

SURVIVAL HINTS

1. Try Nicorette or other smoking substitutes. They can make a big difference when you're trying to quit.
2. Try quitting with a friend. You can encourage each other and share your ups and downs. And sometimes a little competition is a good thing!
3. Scare yourself if nothing else works. There are vast numbers of Web sites and films about the diseases caused by smoking; they can get your attention if you need to be shocked into quitting.

The Fear Factor

Bob Rubell

SEVENTEEN YEARS AGO, I smoked three packs a day—Kools. I did stuff I swore I'd never do, like smoke as soon as I got out of the shower, before breakfast. In the winter, if I ran out of smokes, I'd throw on shorts, sandals, and a T-shirt and run out for more. If I couldn't make it to the store, I smoked the butts. I was hard core.

One day, I woke up spitting blood. And I don't mean a few drops—I mean a lot. There I was in Brooklyn, all alone, as sick as a dog, lying on the couch, and wearing my third blood-soaked T-shirt. My girlfriend, Lynne, in New Jersey, begged me to go to the doctor, but I was too scared. For two days I lay there, no food, no drink. Two days later, the blood finally stopped. I was too weak to eat, but I could drink a little water. I stayed home from work a few days—I was working on Wall Street back then.

Lynne said that because I had gone two days without smoking, I should try for a third, but I could always start again whenever I wanted. One day followed the next, and I didn't smoke for a year. Finally, one year after the blood scare, I went to the doctor and asked for a physical that concentrated on the lungs. He asked why. When I told him, he couldn't believe that I'd waited so long to have a check-up. When the test results came back, my lungs had completely rejuvenated. I was very lucky.

How have I remained smoke-free all these years? A few simple ways. None of my friends are smokers now, and I don't hang out with smokers any more. I play in a band or two, and sometimes I have a drink in smoky bars. Lynne can always tell where I've been because my clothes reek of smoke. But it's not from me. No more coughing, no butts. I'm no longer a smoker.

SURVIVAL HINTS

1. To change your habit, change your venue. If you stay away from places where people smoke, you'll have less of an urge.
2. If none of your friends smoke, you'll have less opportunity yourself, and no one to bum a smoke from. Peer pressure is a good thing sometimes, especially if none of your friends smoke and don't want to be around the filthy habit.
3. It's very helpful to have a supportive significant other, partner, or spouse. A little encouragement never hurts.
4. If you ever cough up blood, consult a doctor right away. Do not wait a year. You might not be as lucky as Bob!

The Surgeon General's Report

Evelyn M. Fazio

IT WAS THE 1960S. I was little, in elementary school, and my father was a smoker. He smoked a couple of packs a day of unfiltered Camels. They had a pyramid and a camel on the package. They were strong. He smoked in the bathroom. We couldn't go in there without an Aqua-Lung after he came out, because we could not breathe because of all the smoke.

Somewhere along the line, my father heard that it was safer to use filters. But in those days, nobody admitted the dangers that cigarettes posed. So to hedge his bets, he switched to filtered Parliaments. They came in a boring box. Just a logo that looked like a checkmark or a chevron, but they still emitted plenty of smoke.

Then came the fateful day. The surgeon general's report was published, and the report said that smoking caused cancer. That pretty much did it for my father. He turned white when the newscaster went into detail, and then he got up and went out of the room. I could hear paper crunching in the next room.

I asked him what he was doing. He said, "I'm throwing out my cigarettes." "Good," I thought. "At least now we would be able to breathe in the bathroom."

Being a kid, I didn't realize how hard it was to quit, especially after decades of smoking. But he did it, and on a dime. He never looked back, either. He did put on a few pounds, mostly because he traded smoking for eating—and just about anything would do. Sometimes he'd walk around munching on celery stalks or carrots, depending on his mood. But often it was a Hershey bar, and you know where that leads.

One day, many years later, a group of us were talking about how they had all quit smoking. Some admitted that they'd done so several times before they finally quit for good. My father said no, not him. He had been scared to death by the surgeon general's report, and his fear was stronger than his addiction.

But that day he revealed one thing that my mother and I had not known: For the first twelve years after he quit, he'd kept an emergency pack of cigarettes in his bathrobe pocket, the one he never wore, which was stuffed into the back of his closet—just in case!

SURVIVAL HINTS

1. Check out www.QuitSmoking.com; you'll find smoking chat boards and all kinds of valuable and practical information on quitting and how to avoid weight gain.
2. If you want to quit, find a strong motivator, and fear can be the best one. When it comes to quitting smoking, I believe that any route is good as long as it works for you.
3. If you are worried about gaining weight when you quit, consider keeping carrot sticks and celery handy so that you'll keep your hand out of the cookie jar. If you gain a few pounds, you'll still be better off healthwise than if you keep smoking. This is a case where vanity really can kill you!

The Wild Ride

Samantha Jones

"I'M READY TO GO," I said to my husband as we ran out the door late to catch a flight to Hawaii. We were on our way to a vacation we had spent years saving for: a three-week stay on the beautiful island of Oahu. "Wait a minute, I forgot my smokes," I said as I ran back into the house to grab them. When you're a smoker, there is no going anywhere without your butts. I rooted around through everything in the house and could not find the carton anywhere. "What could I have possibly done with it?" I asked myself.

My husband—a nonsmoker—walked back into the house and said, "We've gotta go. Were going to miss our flight." Looking at my watch, I knew he was right. There was just enough time to get to the airport and even that was going to be cutting it close. I was in a funk, and an immediate feeling of withdrawal came over me like a large dark cloud.

How could I go all the way to Hawaii without having a smoke? I would never make it. My happy "Let's go on vacation" mood was quickly changing to my "If I don't get a cigarette, I am not going anywhere" mood. My husband drove like an Indy 500 pro to get us to the airport on time. I was holding on to the oh-my-God bar over the passenger window—just to keep from sliding off of my seat. As if my nerves weren't already shot, he had to drive like an maniac, making me want a smoke all the more!

Upon reaching the airport—somehow still in one piece—I said, "I have to find a place to get a pack of smokes." He said, "You don't have time." And I didn't. We made it to the gate with no time to spare, and they were just about to declare us no-shows.

The day I boarded that plane was the day I gave up smoking forever. It had taken me three years to save for this vacation; it could have been paid for three years earlier if I hadn't smoked, and then we almost missed the trip because of my misplaced cigarettes.

It wasn't easy and sometimes it still isn't, but taking yourself out of familiar surroundings, away from your

normal schedule and routine, can make a big difference. Being in Hawaii during my transition period
made quitting that much easier, probably also because
I was relaxed and unstressed. And now, whenever I
want to go back to Hawaii, I just save up some cigarette money and I'm off to the airport.

SURVIVAL HINTS

1. The transition phase from smoker to nonsmoker may
   be difficult, but the freedom you get in return for not
   smoking is wonderful.
2. Think, too, about the money you will save. What better perk and reward for giving up an unhealthy vice!

7

When You Quit
for Your Health

Sanity Quiz

You have just come home from the doctor after being informed that you have a choice: Stop smoking and live or keep smoking and die.

Do you
A. say it's too late for you and keep puffing
B. recognize your situation and try your best to stop
C. light one up and think long and hard about it

If you picked any of these choices, you need to read on and find out how these old pros managed to get scared into quitting!

Scott, the Smoking Survivor

Felina Katz

I'VE KNOWN SCOTT for more than twenty-two years.
We worked together when I was at my first job, and
nearly everything I know about business I learned
from him. He's smart, a graduate of Yale and the
University of Pennsylvania, and one of the finest people I know—a class act.

In 1988, Scott was giving a presentation to the management of our company when he suddenly stopped
talking. I carried on with the presentation, and then
we left the meeting. He told me he'd had a sudden

pain in his neck. I, being known to crack wise on occasion, naturally responded by saying yes, that pain in the neck was from the management meeting and I had a similar one in another part of my anatomy. He shook his head no, pointing to his neck—he really did have a pain.

Scott was a smoker. He always smoked at his desk, usually while chewing gum and tapping his foot as he typed away. He was probably the most successful executive in our division; he booked the best sales increases in the entire corporation, and he did so every year. He also worked long and hard, and when deadlines loomed, he really smoked up a storm.

Scott took his cigarettes everywhere. I recall that he often bounced straight up from his seat at lunch in our company cafeteria, patted down his pockets, and then raced from the room to find a vending machine—he was out of cigarettes once again. We always knew where he was going, but it was still funny each time it happened; it was partly the wide-eyed look of panic on his face and partly the way he zipped out of the cafeteria at breakneck speed, off in search of a fix.

Not very long after the pain in the neck episode, Scott found out he had a growth in his throat and that the doctors were concerned about it. He was to have it scraped off, and then a biopsy would be performed to make sure the growth was nothing serious. I picked him up from the hospital after the procedure, and naturally he had a cigarette.

Soon we got the stunning news that the growth wasn't harmless—it was cancer. Not only that, but after it had been scraped off, it grew right back. It was aggressive. I was in denial, but Scott remained calm. The doctors decided they'd have to remove a vocal chord, but the other side of his throat should be okay. After the surgery, he returned to work. He had lots of medical follow-ups, but only a few months later, there was more stunning news: The doctors had found more cancer, and more surgery was necessary.

He'd be given a tracheotomy, and he'd have to talk by using the air in his throat. It was the end of his smoking days, and it was a drastic method for stopping. He told me that some people still smoked through the holes in their necks, but he was too smart to try anything like that.

The surgery went well, and soon Scott was recovering rapidly. Amazingly, he was still able to talk, albeit with a raspy voice, and much to the surprise of the nursing staff. Before long, he was back at work. He had radiation treatments every morning before work. He looked great, and behaved as if nothing had happened. We were all awed by his cheerful optimism and strength.

Soon the positive effects of not smoking began to show. Now Scott's skin started looking smooth and rosy. He had a spring in his step, too. He told me that food tasted different, and tuna, which he often ate for lunch, was now too fishy for him! And he was moving at high speeds again, just as before, and the rest of us had to pick up our pace to keep up.

Recently, I visited Scott and he looked better than ever. Sixteen years after his surgery, after quitting smoking, he is in perfect health; he walks several miles a day, and nothing slows him down.

Now, I don't think Scott would recommend a tracheotomy and cancer as a means of quitting smoking, but I'm certain that he'd tell you himself not to wait for such a drastic situation before you quit, too! Staying alive and healthy is the best way to survive and stay sane.

Gambling with Life

Ed Stevens

SMOKING IS A GAMBLE, no matter how you look at it. You're gambling with your life and the lives of those around you. Chances are that if you're a smoker and also a parent, your kids are going to end up smoking, too. No matter what you tell them about the bad effects of smoking, if you are still smoking, your advice is meaningless. Monkey see, monkey do. Now risking your own life is one thing, but you are risking the lives of the ones you love most if you don't quit.

Would you put your child in the middle of the street and wait to see if a car hits him? Would you let your child swim with sharks to see if he is attacked?

Would you expose your children to the world's most deadly germs to find out whether they would survive? Of course you wouldn't. Then why would you poison them slowly with second-hand smoke, which will ultimately lead to their first-hand smoking in the end? You are putting more than yourself at risk.

It took me two years to realize this and to stop the smoking madness. I smoked because my parents smoked when I was a youngster. I started out by stealing a few here and there from either Mom or Dad's pack, and then worked my way right up to being a two-pack-a-day cloud. What I didn't realize was that the cloud was now covering my own kids. I was doing to someone else exactly what had been done to me.

If you make smoking a part of your life, you deem it acceptable and are implanting that message into your children's minds. You are telling them it's okay to be a smoker. But it's not okay and you know it isn't. Smokers spend their lives planning to quit. They think about it all the time. But thinking won't solve the problem.

For me, the doctor's words finally put an end to my puffing. He said, "It's simple. Either you quit or you're going to die." Now I was a gambler, and I had gambled on many things in my time. But I wasn't willing to gamble my life and the lives of those around me just to smoke. So that day, I vowed to become a nonsmoker, and I succeeded, for myself and everyone around me.

It's been two years now and I am smokeless. I am also healthier and much happier now that I am no longer dependent upon death in a pack. It wasn't easy. I had my ups and downs, but if you stick to it, you'll get there. It's worth it because there are better things to gamble with than your life.

SURVIVAL HINTS

1. If you won't quit for yourself, do it for the ones you love.
2. Seek outside help when you need it. There are many resources available to smokers, and the Internet is a great place to start.
3. Weigh all your options and set a date to quit, then go for it!

Remembering Dad

Pamela K. Brodowsky

MY DAD SMOKED back when it was Jimmy Dean cool. Now, smoking makes you more of an outcast than an idol. Do you remember when men used to roll packs of smokes up in their T-shirt sleeves? Can you imagine the look someone would get now for doing that? Holy smoke, how things have changed.

I was around smokers and picked up smoking as a bad habit from them. Now don't get me wrong—it was my own fault. You can't blame your smoking on anyone else but yourself. Back then, they didn't know how harmful it was; as a result, many have paid dearly—some with their lives.

My father was one of the some. He didn't die of cancer, though. He died of respiratory failure at sixty-three. One day while he was sitting in a chair watching television, he just stopped breathing. I lost my best friend that day, my father and the grandfather of my children, a man I truly admired and dearly loved.

Now, as I keep a tight rein on my memories of him, I also remember the difficulties and crazy stunts he pulled while trying to quit smoking. He was on oxygen for a few years before he died, and this restricted him to the house somewhat. He no longer drove as a result, and he went out only occasionally. My mother refused to let him smoke and refused to buy him any more cigarettes. She forced him into quitting—or so she thought.

Being the diehard smoker he was, and quite clever, he always found a way to get a cigarette. Whether it was by stealing one from your pack while you went to the bathroom or offering to go into the store on one of his very few trips out, he always managed to find a way. But the day that took the cake was the day he called for a Pizza Hut delivery.

He ordered himself a pizza and a bottle of soda; he also offered the kid a twenty-dollar tip if he would stop on the way and pick him up a couple of packs of smokes. The kid did it. What the hell, it was an easy twenty.

The funny part is that my father was so impressed with his own cleverness that he had to tell my mother the story when she got home. She didn't find it quite so funny and made him give up his stash. After all, a man who needs oxygen shouldn't be smoking. Not only that, but he wouldn't even take out the tube while he was smoking. He's lucky he didn't blow up!

Shortly after that episode, he quit for good. A little too late for him—but not for the rest of us. It's not easy to quit and never will be, so don't kid yourself. But if you want a long and healthy life, you'd be better off quitting now.

SURVIVAL HINTS

1. Rather than waste energy in finding clever ways to cheat, use it to find ways to cope while you quit.
2. It's never too late to start a quit-smoking program. Find one that works for you and stick to it. If you don't know where to begin or what program to begin with, visit the Web site for the American Cancer Society, or similar sites, for more information. Don't wait until it's too late.

The Price of Smoking

Willis Wong

HAVE YOU EVER THOUGHT about the true costs of being a smoker? I didn't until I quit, but let me give you some financial facts that may inspire you to quit, too. Everyone should have incentives, especially when trying to quit smoking.

Let's take a look at just the initial costs. A pack of smokes ranges anywhere from $4 to $7. Most smokers smoke anywhere from one to three packs a day. A one-pack habit on the high end will cost $7 a day and a three-pack habit $21 a day. That means a one-pack-a-day smoker spends $210 a month to kill himself, and a three-pack-a-day smoker spends $630 a month.

Can't you think of anything better to do with that money? I don't even want to tell you what you are spending a year, because when I look back it still makes me sick to think about the amount of cash I spent on cigarettes. Ah, hell, I'll tell you anyway. For the one-packer, an annual price tag of $2,520; and for the three-packer, $7,560. What a waste of money. You're paying to poison yourself. You realize that, don't you?

Now for $630 a month, you could drive a nice car or maybe even buy a second home. Neither purchase will deteriorate at the rate your body will if you don't stop smoking. Oh, you say, you already drive a nice car and you already have a second home. But you won't be around long to enjoy either if you don't stop smoking.

Money is no object. You just want to live high on the hog. But you won't be living so well when you are hooked up to the respirator that will have to breathe for you if you don't stop smoking.

It may not be easy to quit, but neither will your life be easy if you don't stop smoking. The longer you smoke, the worse the damage to your body. You can use excuse after excuse. I have said and heard them all. It took me a long time to quit, but I did it and I was a three-pack-a-day puff-house. So get off your butt and get off the butts and buy yourself a nice new shiny red car or a house away from home. Nothing is worth the price you'll pay if you don't recognize the cost of smoking.

SURVIVAL HINTS

1. Do it for yourself.
2. Don't pay the ultimate price.
3. Buy yourself something nice with all that extra cash.

How the World's Smallest Smoker Quit

Evelyn M. Fazio

SHE WAS A VERY TINY LITTLE GIRL, about the age of five. The second youngest of seven, she weighed only five pounds at her premature birth, and somehow she survived despite the odds. Her second oldest brother, Joe, was in the navy. It was 1926, and he came home on leave with a bunch of his friends.

The sailors were everywhere in the big old house, having a ball playing cards and smoking up a storm. The little girl was surrounded by all those big handsome guys in their white uniforms—the house was full of them—enjoying all the merriment and commotion.

The smoking itself was fascinating. The sailors were blowing smoke rings, and making smoke come out of their nostrils. It looked like such fun, and kind of exciting, too.

When nobody was watching, the little girl stole two cigarettes out of the nearest pack and sneaked out to meet her friend, Minette. A block or so away, Minette's backyard abutted the synagogue. The two girls decided this would be a good place to try out their newfound treasures. There they stood, two very small girls, lighting cigarettes behind the synagogue. Soon, they were coughing and gagging, but were undeterred in their mission to be cool like those sailors back at the house.

Just at that moment, Mrs. Sussman looked out the window. There she saw two little girls amid their little cloud of smoke. Mrs. Sussman's eyes widened in surprise. The girls were puffing away, and the smaller of the two, her daughter's best friend, was making smoke come out of her nose. Her own daughter, Minette, was right there beside her, puffing away along with her, eyes red and tearing, too.

The tinier puffer was turning a strange shade of green, like the color of celery. Mrs. Sussman hurried around the block to see her neighbor, Theresa, the other girl's mother, and told her what she'd seen.

Both mothers shook their heads. What had gotten into these mischievous girls of theirs to try such a thing at so young an age? It was the Roaring Twenties, but the children were only five!

The little cigarette thief came home. She was green. She was sick. She was scolded. Mom is eighty-four now, and since that day so long ago she has never smoked again. I suppose you could say that a lesson learned early is a lesson learned well.

The Other War America Won

Keith R. Taylor

THE TIDE HAS CLEARLY TURNED in the smoking war, and smoking clearly lost. Even Rush Limbaugh jumped ship and abandoned the implacable smoking hangers-on. The tobacco companies are now all conglomerates and sell healthful stuff such as Oreos and other delights to make up for the shortfall in tobacco sales. The main body of American smokers has been routed. As for the remaining stalwarts, Philip Morris is now apologizing to them while helping them complete the job of ruining their health.

But tobacco isn't dead. Our good old institution of telling kids how smoking makes them look cool has shifted to Asia, where different youngsters can puff away and say good-bye to childhood while greeting a shortened adulthood.

Like so many wars, this one was won or lost (depending on your view) incrementally. First, we had smoking and nonsmoking sections in restaurants. That was fine in restaurants where the stale air tended to stay in one place because of poor air circulation. Otherwise, the nonsmokers just had to cough and bear it.

Then baseball joined the parade. The Marlboro man came down from the stadiums, presumably to wheeze and cough. Not satisfied with putting actors out of work, the forces of good health made entire stadiums smokeless, a move even more heretical than Phillip Wrigley's introduction of Ladies Day.

The love affair between tobacco and baseball is a long and colorful one. My special hero, Mickey Mantle, was a switch hitter in baseball and in smoking. R. J. Reynolds paid the great Yankee slugger to tout Camels, even though he didn't smoke. When that was reported, the Mick simply started smoking. Old Number Seven hit them so far that he didn't need to run much. Later, Number Seven endorsed a product to help smokers kick the habit. He finally kicked the habit himself, not long before he died of cancer.

Ronald Reagan himself got me to try Chesterfields when I was a mere tot. The future president looked dashing in the magazine ads. But I was fickle. Bert Wilson, the Chicago Cubs' announcer, touted Old Golds, and that was good enough for me. I hacked and coughed my way through many a pack.

So I smoked. Lord, did I ever! Continuing with the habit picked up in my childhood, I approached my sixth decade by putting away three packs a day—it would have been even more if I had thrown back a few beers to go along with them. I suffered all the slings and arrows my smoking friends of today receive from the sanctimonious nonsmokers.

Thus, when I gave up the habit in 1979, I promised myself I wouldn't join the parade of do-gooders who wanted to decide what other folks did with their own lives. I simply didn't want to be a pain in the ass about it. Not a smoker alive hadn't already been besieged by the mountains of data. Even those folks banished to the cold outdoors to smoke knew about the dangers of lighting up. What good would one more complainer do? "Live and let live" would be my motto.

Then a couple of years after I kicked the habit for the last time, two of my friends died of lung cancer. Both had been heavy smokers. Both knew the dangers of cigarettes. My daughter's mother-in-law, Olive, was diagnosed with the disease and died within a few months. She has missed out on three terrific grand-daughters.

Her husband, a guy they called Moose, was a gnarled, rough, tough, retired navy boatswain's mate. He was one of the early underwater demolition team guys. Veterans of that elite group spoke about him with awe. Moose was a legend. He had survived dangerous missions in World War II, Korea, and some places he wouldn't talk about. He died of respiratory illness and heart disease a few years after his wife's death.

Moose's funeral was a moving ceremony—I always get emotional when they play Taps. As they say, it gets me in the Pall Malls. The chapel was filled with old shipmates, many of whom had tears in their eyes as they hurried out of the building to light up another cigarette.

Robbie, an insurance client of mine, had, like me, given up smoking. We exchanged ideas. I had traded one compulsion for another; I had become a runner and was training for my first marathon.

Robbie proudly shared the feeling that the worst part of her addiction was over. Food was starting to taste good again. Perhaps she, too, would take up running to avoid gaining weight. The money not spent on her habit would go towards a really fantastic trip. When I pointed out that the premiums on her life insurance policy would soon be cut significantly, she was delighted—more money for the trip. The discount, however, would not go into effect until she had been off cigarettes for a year.

But she never made that trip. A few weeks later, she called me. When I asked the perfunctory question, "How are you, Robbie?" She replied, "Not so hot, Keith. It seems that I didn't quit smoking soon enough. The doctor just told me I have lung cancer."

Robbie was barely forty; she had a right to expect to live another thirty years or more. I mumbled, "Maybe they've caught it in time."

No. Robbie paid her higher smokers' premiums for just a few more months, and then she died. The insurance turned out to be a good buy after all.

My resolve to live and let live was being tested. Those happy folks in the magazine ads somehow didn't seem to represent Olive, who didn't live long enough to see her namesake, or Robbie, who missed the entire second half of her life.

But someone will always spoil the fun. Isn't that always the way it is? C. Everett Koop, the former surgeon general, claimed that nicotine is more addictive than heroin and cocaine. Is it? Well, Moose managed to give up the habit only for a week or so after he lost his wife of thirty-six years to cancer.

I don't want to be a pain in the ass. I promise I won't make a disparaging remark to the smokers huddled outside buildings, but forgive me if I don't get in the way of the war on smokers. I don't like wars, but it looks like we finally have one worth fighting.

An Enemy No Bigger than My Little Finger

Robert White

NOW THAT I THINK ABOUT IT, maybe I should say I started smoking in the womb and quit for the first time at birth. Both my parents smoked. My father never quit; but my mother stopped when she was nearly sixty, after forty years of unfiltered Camels. While I was away at college, I decided to try cigarettes just to see if I'd like them. I did.

My mother's nickname was Pill, bestowed on her by her older sister's infant son in his attempts to say his Aunt Mildred's name. As a smart-assed young adult, I starting using the nickname Mom was given in her younger, babysitting days. My revival of the name failed at its intended purpose, which was to pester and annoy. It's not always easy for an only son, and youngest child, to get under a mother's skin.

Using the name became symbolic of the closeness of the bond between us. I used it when I introduced her to friends and acquaintances; and for me, and for most of them, she was Pill for the rest of her life.

Now Pill was one of those people who believed that if she had accomplished something, that same goal should be attainable for everyone else. I remember getting annoyed with her for this attitude on the few occasions we discussed the topic of kicking the habit, but one particular comment she made has stayed with me to this day.

She decided, once she had made up her mind to quit, that she would not allow herself to be beaten by something no bigger than her baby finger. By her own reckoning, giving up cigarettes was one of the most difficult projects she had ever undertaken. She got little encouragement from my father; indeed, she endured a fair amount of ridicule, yet her resolve never faltered.

When my partner and I had been together for thirteen years, we moved into a two-family house with my mother. This move was in accordance with her wish to spend her final years in the protective presence of her family. Dad had been dead for eight years, and my mother had needed that time alone to arrive at the point where she could move on. She chose to live with us rather than with any of my sisters and their families.

We had the good fortune to find a place that suited all our needs well. Everyone was under the same roof, but each household enjoyed its separate and reasonably ample space. We lived upstairs, Mom lived down. Older people think about stairs. I was greatly comforted to know first-hand how my mother was faring, and I was glad to be close by should she need any help.

The inevitable decline began with a stroke in 1986 and reached its inescapable end on my birthday in 2003. For the final five years or so, my partner's job had required him to spend about every second week in New York City. This meant that I had my mother, our house, two parrots, a job, and a partner, when he was home, all competing for my attention. Those were not the best of times to quit smoking, even had I tried.

A week after we buried Pill, my partner learned that he would be required to relocate permanently to New York City, but his company was willing to postpone the move until the following year, when I would be eligible for retirement. Throughout that year, I had a lot of adjusting to accomplish. Radical changes had occurred in my life, and more were on the horizon.

I began to think about how the move to a new city, essentially the beginning of a new existence, would be an appropriate time to rid myself of a bad old habit. I bought nicotine patches and put them away. I wanted them within easy reach for that day when I might find strength, courage, and resolve at the same time.

A trip to the dentist chose that day for me. A couple of weeks before our scheduled move, I went for a routine cleaning and checkup. The doctor found a white spot on my throat. He told me that, although he had never had a biopsy come back positive for a serious condition, he strongly recommended that I have the spot checked out as soon as possible. He gave me the name of a specialist, a prescription slip with a description of the problem, a drawing of what he had seen, and his promise that he would call ahead to ensure that the specialist fit me into his schedule without delay.

Two or three days later, the specialist's examination found that the spot was nearly gone. He was so confident that I had no reason to worry that he did not even do a biopsy of the affected tissue. I read this reprieve as an omen, my cue that the day of reckoning had arrived.

I took the patches from the closet and put one on. I did very well without cigarettes for a while, but the ever increasing stress of the move broke my resolve. At first, I tried having one or two a day to tame the beast of my cravings just enough to make it manageable; but by the time we arrived in New York, I had relapsed completely.

For several years my family had made Pill's birthday the one occasion when we all gathered to celebrate together. Pill loved it back in scenic, bucolic Kentucky, where she'd lived with my father, especially when she was surrounded by all her family. For this reason, even after she was gone, we decided to gather there in her honor each year at around the same time; and, before my move to New York, my sisters made me promise to travel back to Kentucky each year for the event.

Through all the farewell gatherings and dinners held in our honor before our departure for New York, I had represented myself as a reformed smoker. No one back home knew that ultimately I had not succeeded in my attempt to quit. I found myself faced with the prospect of going back home for the reunion as a failure in this endeavor.

Of course, I had been kicking myself repeatedly for my weakness and had been thinking constantly about renewing my effort. Dieters obsess about food; those who would kick the habit of smoking think constantly about cigarettes. I was determined to prove myself. Out came the patches again a few days before the trip back home.

Somehow I made it through that weekend; and, even more astonishing, reunion time this year, only a month away, brings with it my first smoke-free anniversary.

Remarkably, I have had few serious cravings; and I have been able to push those few away with thoughts of some compelling reasons why I need not smoke. My partner is one. We've seen twenty-eight years together, happy over all, and predominantly healthy. I want to keep it this way for as long as possible.

Then I must consider my parrots, my little green children, to whose care I have committed. They can live for a very long time, and have human life spans. Quite likely they will outlive me as it is; but I owe it to them to be around for them for as long as possible, to try to postpone the trauma and disruption to their lives that my disappearance will cause.

These thoughts and the idea of a new start in a new place have helped keep me sane and strong against the attacks of cravings. The real secret of success here results from the happy convergence of many factors.

Whatever the reasons may be, I am hopeful and reasonably confident that I have vanquished at last that enemy no bigger than my little finger.

8

When Using Substitutes for Smoking

Sanity Quiz

You quit smoking two weeks ago. It hasn't been easy, but so far you've made it. Today is a bit rougher for you than most. Your boss is on your back, your kids are riding you, and your husband is a bigger pain than usual. Your cravings are getting to the uncontrollable stage.

Do you
A. relieve your stress by eating an entire box of Oreos
B. run to Krispy Kreme and eat a dozen donuts before you go back to the office
C. go out to lunch and eat seven hot dogs, then feel sick for the remainder of the day
D. totally lose it and go to the nearest store for a pack of butts

No matter which of these answers you selected, you need to read on and find out exactly how these folks substituted something else—anything else—rather than smoke. They're the experts, so we'll let them tell you about it themselves.

Beating Uncle Phil

Dralyn Veech

I HAD BEEN SMOKING for many years when I finally decided to quit again, and for good (I believe this was attempt number four). But first it was necessary to keep reminding myself of the reason I was doing this painful task.

Mental notes on reasons for quitting:

A. it's a smelly habit
B. it's an expensive habit
C. it's a dirty habit
D. it's bad for your health
E. it's a way to escape Uncle Phil's clutches

Uncle Phil is my name for my former habitual use of Philip Morris products.

Luckily, at the point in my life when I quit smoking for good, I was an ardent home exerciser and did a lot of cardio and weight training. I pushed my cardio workouts, thinking the increased need for oxygen would eventually win out over my need for nicotine. Surprisingly, it worked! My end-of-workout cigarette was a visual that helped me get through my exercise tape routine, but in the process I wore myself out and didn't even want the cigarette by the time I had finished the workout. By this time, I was working out six days a week, and smoking less and less. I had no free time in which to smoke, and I was getting into great shape at the same time.

Another thing that worked for me was to breathe deeply instead of reaching for a smoke. Doing this frequently gave me a feeling of being both light-headed *and* euphoric, probably from the increased oxygen my body was not used to receiving. So try deep breathing; it worked for me.

Sitting on my hands was another technique that worked, especially in the winter, when the weather turned cold and my fingers became perpetual ice cubes. It kept my hands occupied and still, lessening the nervous need to hold a cigarette in my fingers, and giving me warm hands at the same time. To this day, I often catch myself sitting on my hands, and I highly recommend it to help control the need for cigarettes. This technique also works well when you're dieting.

It's been more than six years since my last puff on a cigarette, and I hope to remain a nonsmoking smoker for the rest of my life. (I choose this designation because, in my opinion, a smoker is never an ex-smoker or a nonsmoker; never say never really does apply to smoking.)

Not smoking is a clean and guilt-free, not to mention cheaper, way to live. My lungs enjoy the added oxygen, and my home smells more like garlic these days than Uncle Phil's parlor.

Staying sane is staying healthy and in control; it is also no longer being Uncle Phil's girl. I think I've finally beaten him into submission at last!

SURVIVAL HINTS

1. Try deep breathing as a substitute for puffing on a weed.
2. Keep your hands occupied with whatever helps; try knitting or even twirling a pencil. And, of course, you can also sit on your hands.
3. Keep snacks such as carrots, pretzel sticks, celery stalks, and other long, thin foods that will replace the feeling of a cigarette in your hand.

Big Betty's Snack Attack

Melanie Hughes

BIG BETTY WAS MY NEIGHBOR. But we didn't call her Big Betty until she decided to quit smoking. In fact, Betty was a rather slim and attractive woman when I first met her. I don't ever think she ate three meals a day. She was a stick. One day while we were having tea, which we did every Tuesday, she announced she was giving up the filthy smoking habit in pursuit of a healthier life. She had been smoking for more than twenty years and had had enough. I commended Betty on her efforts. "That's great," I said.

I gave up smoking some years ago, and I knew a little encouragement could go a long way. I told Betty that if she needed anything, she should feel free to ask. A few weeks went by and I noticed that Betty was getting a bit thicker around the middle. Not only that, but now our tea on Tuesday had turned into cakes and tea, and sometimes cakes, sandwiches, and tea. Betty was clearly using snacks to fill her need to smoke—snacks that she had never eaten before, but was now substituting for cigarettes.

Because of Betty's delightful substitutions, I, too, was getting a bit fat around the waistline. She didn't want to eat alone and insisted that I join her. Luckily, I was only a weekly participant in this feast. This went on for weeks until finally I had to point out to Betty just how large she had grown and that even these once-a-week treats were beginning to affect my own weight.

This wasn't an easy thing for me to do, and it wasn't easy for Betty to hear how she was succeeding in one area while causing herself a whole new problem in another. After some tears and a few good laughs, we decided that we both had to cut down on the snacks and that Big Betty had to find something other than food to feed her need.

Luckily, Betty did just that. Now, rather than stuff herself full of fattening snacks, she eats baby carrots like a bunny. They're healthy and fill that hand-to-mouth habit that smokers are so used to. As for the fat, we both lost what we had put on, but it took us twice the time, and it was only half the fun!

SURVIVAL HINTS

1. Most smokers will gain weight during the quitting stages, but it's usually less than ten pounds. Dealing with one issue at a time is crucial to the success of your being smoke free, so focus on quitting first.
2. Focusing on staying healthy rather than on what you weigh can aid you in your battle to stay smoke free as well as slim.
3. Eat plenty of fruits, vegetables, and nuts to help cut your cigarette craving, and watch out for high-fat snacks so you don't end up like Betty.

Diary of a Smoker

Anika Green

Day One

Today I have decided to quit smoking. Well, that is not entirely true. I have been quitting for years, but today is the day that I am actually starting the real thing. I woke up this morning and didn't light up. Instead, I drank my coffee and bit my finger nails. Until this morning, I had beautiful finger nails. Now I have little stubs where my nails once were.

When I went to work, I actually got in the car without lighting up. A major accomplishment. I normally smoke three cigarettes before I arrive at the office. I even know which roads I pass when it's time to have one, so today I took another route to work.

Supper was delicious, and the after-dinner cigarette that I didn't have was even better. Dessert tasted like never before. Bedtime came and went without a smoke.

Day Two

Today I was a little angry and had a headache. I had light cravings, but I know deep down that this is what is best for me. My fingers are bleeding because of my nail-biting; I look like an advertisement for Band-Aids. My kids are driving me nuts and my husband is annoying me more than usual. When I look at my pack of smokes, I make myself look away; I tell myself that this is best for both my family and me.

Work was more stressful than usual. The senior partners were making demands on all of us. I really wanted a smoke—needed a smoke—but somehow I made it through without one. I'm proud of myself.

Dinner was ready when I got home. A happy surprise that gave me a minute to unwind. I had a glass of wine, my first without a cigarette. I feel better now.

Day Three

I'm really starting to crave. The nicotine must be leaving my body. I'm happy I haven't given in. It's been a trying few days, but I'm determined to make it.

Instead of going to work today, I called in sick and decided to spend the day at the beach. It was a hard day for me and I knew that taking myself out of the stressful daily routine would help me relax and not smoke. The day soon became easy. I didn't think about how much I wanted a smoke, and instead I thought about the beauty of the ocean.

I went home early and prepared a reward dinner. I deserved it and so did my family. Quitting smoking has now become a bit easier.

Day Four

I was at the breaking point today. I really wanted to smoke. It's consuming my every thought. Just knowing I can't have one is clearly driving me nuts. I have a migraine. My body is going through withdrawal. My kids won't let up. My husband is irritated with me because of my lack of patience. My world is falling apart. I'm having a hard time holding it together and I want to scream.

When I went outside and deeply inhaled fresh air, I felt better. I distanced myself from everyone today because I knew it was going to be a hard day. This was the only way to go.

Day Five

I've made it five days without a smoke. Today I woke up and the craving had lessened. I wasn't dying to pollute myself anymore. I can do this. I've made it this far. My headache has gone. I'm no longer angry. I decided to take the kids to the park. They deserve it for putting up with me.

We went out for pizza tonight. The day was another smoke-free success. I feel good. My family is as happy for me as I am for myself.

One Year Later

I am still smoke free. It took me a long time to adjust, but only the first week was really difficult. There have been lots of benefits. My skin looks healthier. Food tastes better. My teeth are whiter. I can run and play with my children without becoming short of breath. My house no longer smells like an ashtray. Life is good.

SURVIVAL HINTS

1. Don't say you're quitting until you are ready. You have to be dedicated and serious about making this life change. And remember, it's not easy for anyone.
2. Take yourself out of pressing situations that would normally cause you to smoke. Your temptations will decrease and your success rate will increase.
3. Reward yourself for every day you make it through without giving in. Every smokeless day is a great accomplishment.
4. Don't give up even when you slip up.

Putting Your Butt on the Line

Hector Hernandez

I'M QUITTING, I'M SICK OF IT. Everywhere you go anymore if you're a smoker, people see you as some kind of leper. You can't smoke in restaurants; you can't smoke in bars, especially in New York City. Hotels are even doing away with their smoking rooms. What's going on? I even heard recently that California is trying to forbid smoking on the beach. Now come on—that's insanity.

Anyhow, I couldn't care less what other people think. That's not why I'm quitting. I'm giving it up because everything this habit involves is a giant pain. Every time you go anywhere, you have to take your smokes with you. If you're traveling for any distance, you have to check your supply. When you smoke too many, you end up nauseated and quickly have to eat something, anything, to get rid of the feeling. Smoking causes all sorts of health problems, not to mention what it does to the way you look. Yellow teeth, bad skin, a collection of lip wrinkles. I don't want to go there.

I've thought long and hard about quitting, and finally came to the conclusion that you just have to do it. Don't question it. Just do it. You can complain later. In fact, chances are you will be complaining all the way through the withdrawal stages anyway, so don't put off until tomorrow what you can do today. Find another habit—one that you can enjoy in public without fear of reprisal.

In place of smoking, I took up beer drinking and butt scratching. I now find them quite a comfortable compromise, and what the hell, it works. I have not yet heard anyone in any restaurant or bar complain about it yet. Here and there I get a few stares, but not one person yet has asked me to put my real butt out.

SURVIVAL HINTS

1. Find another habit and make sure it's a healthier one and that it will improve your life. Replacing your smoking habit with another that you enjoy as much or more will help to ease the strain of quitting.
2. Don't wait. Get started on a quit-smoking program today, because the sooner you quit, the better off and the healthier you'll be.

9

When Someone Helps You Quit

Sanity Quiz

You've decided to quit smoking. Immediately after you made your decision, you announce it to all your family members, coworkers, and casual acquaintances who've been complaining for years about *your* smoking. You will finally be free of the dirty filthy habit, and hope this will get them all off your back. Unfortunately, the message backfires and now all of the above are working overtime to make sure you never smoke again. Their constant nagging is making you so crazy, it's now twice as hard to stay smoke free.

Do you
A. thank them all for their support, but tell them to mind their own damn business
B. tell them they are driving you nuts and their nagging's the reason you quit in the first place
C. take up smoking cigars—the really stinky ones
D. run out, buy a carton, and smoke like you never smoked before

If you answered yes to any of these questions, read on. Our experts will help you survive all this "help." They did, after all!

Clockwork

Pamela K. Brodowsky

WANT TO QUIT SMOKING? Get yourself a two-year-old.

Know how kids are like phone magnets? You could be sitting there for hours without saying a word and the kids act as if you were invisible. But pick up the phone, and they are stuck to you in a split second. They must have some kind of invisible phone-sensing mechanism.

My two-year-old son, who refuses to be potty-trained, has this same sensing mechanism, yet his works not only when I talk on the phone but also every time I light a cigarette. And instead of bothering me, or just screaming in my ear, he poops in his pants, which actually is a bit more of a bother. I light up, he makes a deposit. It's guaranteed. He could be in another room when I slowly and ever so quietly retrieve the cigarette from the pack. As soon as the lighter ignites, here comes the pooping machine.

It took me a while to realize there was a pattern here. But as soon as I did, I began trying to hide my smoking. And it was costing me a small fortune, too. I smoked maybe a third of every cigarette I lit, and next thing you know, I was changing a diaper.

So to save some money, and actually smoke a cigarette without having to clean a crappy diaper in the middle of it, I began closet-smoking. I mean literally in-the-closet smoking. It worked for a while, but soon my son figured out where I had gone. And then he went right back to bringing me his odiferous gifts.

You might ask why I didn't just wait until I had finished my cigarette before I changed him. Well, I will tell you why. Because with my son, a dirty diaper quickly turns into the "load in your pants dance," and if the diaper is not removed promptly, it then turns into wall art or, at times, even body paint. There is no waiting period for junior.

After about three months of being plagued by the two-foot poop-meister, I knew I had to throw in the dipey wipe. I just couldn't take the struggle anymore.

My cigarette consumption had been cut down to almost nothing anyway, so I figured I'd go for it. It took me three weeks to get past the cravings, but they came and finally went. Now I've been smoke-free for more than a year.

The funny thing about it is that two weeks after I quit, my pooping machine got the hang of potty training and has been diaper-free ever since. It really was just like clockwork!

SURVIVAL HINTS

1. If you can't quit for yourself, then at least quit for your kids. Smoking harms not only your health and well-being but the health and well-being of those around you. It's been *proven* that secondary smoke causes cancer.
2. Not smoking sets a good example for your children, and it's a fact that most smokers' children end up smoking. Why take a chance with their health?
3. Quitting smoking also comes with its immediate benefits. Your food will taste better, your breathing will improve, and your sense of smell will increase.
4. Reward yourself. Buy yourself some flowers, eat something tasty. But don't smoke.

Trade-Off

William Talbott

MY WIFE AND I wanted to have a baby. We tried for years without succeeding. Finally we went to the doctor. He said my smoking was causing my sperm count to decline and therefore it was hard for us to conceive. I realized that I could no longer be a smoker. Of course, the decision to quit was easier than the actual quitting, but that was the landmark day. It's also a significant day because it was the day my wife turned into a nymphomaniac.

"Well, that's it," she said. "I told you it was your smoking that was causing us the problem. That combined with those skimpy slingshot underwear you wear, no wonder we're not pregnant."

"You're not pregnant because your doctor has you believing that you should give it to me only once a month, supposedly to make the little guys stronger. And just for your information, 'we're' doesn't work with pregnant. You, my dear, get pregnant, not me. I just help."

"If that's what you call it," she shot back. "Think of it any which way you will, Bill, but your smoking days are over. I want a baby now, not when I'm fifty." On and on she went, lighting into me as if it were all my fault. What are the chances of getting pregnant when you have sex once a month? Only about one in thirty.

Instead of keeping up with the quarrel, and most likely loosing the argument, in the end I just gave in. But what I didn't realize was that when the doctor pronounced my smoking to be the cause of our infertility, my wife decided that his first theory, that we should only have sex once a month, went out the window. And then she made up for lost time.

I hadn't had a smoke in two days; it was rough, but I was handling it. And then it happened. That night when I came home from work, my wife was half naked and waiting. She tore into me like a lioness with a fresh kill. I was exhausted, and this went on for days.

We went from once in thirty days to twenty-nine times in less than a week. Those seemed like better odds to me, but I didn't know how long we could keep up this rate of mating.

My urge to smoke came back with my indecision about how to tell my wife she was killing me and that she had to calm down. About five weeks into this sexual frenzy, my wife announced she was pregnant. Hallelujah, peace at last! I was happy for her, happy for us, and happy for my little me. But then the fear of no more sex came over me. What was my sex life going to be like? Was this the end? Sex was the only thing keeping me away from smoking, and I had put far too much effort (in more ways than one!) into quitting to falter now.

Luckily for me, my wife never lost the urge, but she did slow down to a comfortable rate. We both remained steadfast, and I stayed on my journey to quitting. Our daughter is five now, and we have a set of twins on the way. I guess you could say it was a good trade-off: I screwed my way to abstaining from smoking.

SURVIVAL HINTS

1. Try doing something physical in place of smoking. You're not going to want a cigarette while you are jogging or doing sit-ups or "other" enjoyable activities.
2. Trade-offs are a good way to reward yourself for not smoking. Find something else you enjoy and use it as an incentive, especially if you can do it with a partner!

Smokers Are Stubborn

Jaime Alesandro

IT WAS TIME. Time to quit. Give up the yellow teeth. The bad breath. The smoky stale odor that permeated every piece of clothing I owned. Time to move on, to be healthier instead of careless. After all, my fortieth birthday was approaching, and I wasn't as spry as I used to be.

Despite hearing for years about the effects smoking can have on our bodies, we smokers are stubborn and refuse to believe that we will become a casualty of our own vice. Stubbornness is a trait all smokers have in common. It's natural. If you're a smoker, you're a mule. No ifs, ands, or buts.

Butts, did I say butts? I could really go for one right now. A deep drag of those toxins into my lungs. Oh, how I miss it. My fingers have finally returned to their normal color—they were kind of yellow because the nicotine had stained them over the years. At least I was color-coordinated: My fingers matched the color of my teeth.

Smoking truly does bad things to your skin. And, yeah, you need a thick skin to weather the abuse you are going to give yourself during the stages of quitting. Not to mention the abuse you will have to take from others. Unintentional, of course. I mean how the hell are they supposed to know that you are on edge, and that everything they say or do, right down to the way they are looking at you, is going to drive you nuts? How are they supposed to know that you would like to rip every hair out of their heads with your now non-smoking hands? How are they supposed to know that you are as sick of them as you are of trying to quit this filthy habit? Maybe your tone of voice should have been their first hint. Or that you refuse to talk with them at all anymore. Maybe you need to come right out and stick a sign on your back that says, "Caution, nonsmoker in progress. Stay back, get off my back, and don't come back."

Trying to convey the hardships of quitting smoking to a lifelong nonsmoker is almost impossible. They say ridiculous things; for example: "Just don't smoke."

"Just don't buy them anymore. It's as simple as that."
Or: "How hard can it be?" That's like telling a druggie
to "Just say no." Come on now, do you really believe
that? People who have never smoked should really
keep their two cents to themselves. They have no idea
what it's like, and there is no smoker trying to quit
who wants advice from them anyway. If they want to
show sympathy for your cause, they can do it from a
distance. They are safer that way in the long run.

Quitting smoking is a long-term proposal. It's not
like you quit for a week and it's over. It's a constant
battle, a war, if you will. And you are the only one
fighting it. But if you give in, you have to admit defeat.
And being our usual stubborn selves, giving in is something we as smokers should not do. That is why you
hear so many smokers going around saying that they
need to quit or that they have to quit. Or, yeah, I'm
quitting on Monday. As if they are in control. It's a
bunch of baloney. Either you're doing it or you're not.
It's up to you. Because smokers are stubborn!

SURVIVAL HINTS

1. Quitting is a long haul but well worth the rewards of
   a healthy and long life.
2. Each smokeless day is a successful day. Reward yourself appropriately.
3. Bribe yourself with a treat that you really enjoy.

Quitting's a No-Brainer!

Ellen P. Sander

EVEN AS A CHILD I always hated smoking. Both my parents smoked and my brother started as soon as he was considered old enough. I, on the other hand, tried everything to make them stop. I tried hiding their cigarettes, but the wrath I encountered was too scary. What I learned from this experience was that unless people are seriously motivated, they will not kick this habit. My father was never able give it up. Even after his first heart attack, he still used to sneak his cigarettes. Sadly it finally got the best of him and I lost my father very early. He didn't even make it to my wedding, and he died when he was only fifty-nine. I was very angry with him for a long time.

My mother was finally motivated by her second husband. She was easily influenced by the men in her life. He was totally against her smoking, and when she was sixty she gave it up cold turkey. She was hostile at first, but eventually she calmed down. However, I was always amused when she tried to inhale second-hand smoke. Talk about desperate measures. But she never did smoke again and I was very proud of her.

My brother is a case by himself. He is a walking miracle. He has gone through so many surgeries and procedures for his heart that you would think the man would learn his lesson. However, it took till his fifties for him to finally quit, and I still suspect that he sneaks one now and then. Like father, like son. Both pigheaded (and I mean that in the most loving way).

Now for my story. College was a bad influence on me: I picked up smoking.

I wasn't a serious smoker. Instead, I smoked socially. It's amazing what we do to fit in. I was still smoking when I finished college and when I met my future husband. He was also a smoker, but not a heavy one. Some time into our relationship, we both came down with a nasty bronchial infection. We stopped smoking while we were sick and decided not to pick it up again. We were doing well till the week before our wedding. My fiancé got prenuptial jitters and started smoking again. He promised that he would quit again after all the craziness had settled down. I understood and tolerated the ashtray kisses.

The wedding came and went and so did the honeymoon. The smoking continued and I was becoming upset. He needed to be motivated, and fast. After some serious consideration, I decided to give him the ultimate motivation. Either he stopped smoking or my "wifely duties" would cease. We were a newly married couple. The choice was a no-brainer.

We are still happily married after almost twenty-eight years, and we have two beautiful daughters. Motivation is a wonderful thing.

10

Through Your
Triggers and Cravings

Sanity Quiz

You've been smoke free for five weeks. Today you are hosting a large gala for your daughter's engagement. The entire family and all your friends will attend. Half your guests are smokers, and the other half are the relatives from hell. How will you prepare your nonsmoking self for the added stress to come?

Do you
A. run out to the store and buy all the gum you can find
B. buy a pack of smokes just in case you can't take it
C. ask your family and friends to limit themselves to one smoking area so that you can easily stay far away from it
D. stick close to all the smokers so that you can inhale their second-hand smoke without giving in and lighting up yourself

No matter which answer you chose, you're in good company. Find out how these quitters coped in all kinds of tempting, resolve-threatening circumstances.

Swimming with the Current

Brunhilde Goebbel

I'VE ALWAYS BEEN a strong-willed person, so when I finally decided to quit smoking once and for all, I had to do it without the help of patches, gum, pills, lozenges, or hypnosis. You know my type, the kind of freak who sets her mind to something and, damn it, she's going to succeed no matter what. And even though I winced at the knowledge that quitting smoking was going to be as hard as kicking heroin, which, I'd heard, had similar withdrawal and personality-altering side effects, my experience was going to be a natural process, one similar to natural childbirth or organic vegetarianism. It was indeed going to be a war that I was prepared to win—or die trying to win.

I decided that I'd declare my war on Sunday and start the week off free of smoke. So on Saturday night, just before bed, I took my last drag from a Marlboro and woke up on Sunday morning ready to reload. But I couldn't—I was at war. Thirty minutes after I was supposed to be fueled up with nicotine, my fingers started tingling, my lips turned a light shade of blue, I was gasping for smoke, and my veins ran cold. The feeling was similar to being drunk because I couldn't control my body, and what I couldn't control was not supposed to be happening! I knew that nothing was going to make sense to me during the days and weeks ahead. But I didn't know that I would become a slapstick comedy, a physical hilarity to everyone else.

Because I love the beach, I was aware of the undertow, or riptide, the fierce current that pulls you under the water and quickly casts you out to sea. Well, the lifeguards advise you to swim with the killer current, not against it, or you'll surely drown. With this metaphor in mind, I recognized what was happening to me and embraced my withdrawal symptoms, just as I would a killer current, and tried to swim with it instead of against it. That's how I won. Let me explain.

Imagine needles prickling every inch of your skin and extremities on your body, and feeling the need to squeeze each needle individually. That's how I felt for a week. So to me, swimming upstream meant taking off my shoes and pinching my toes one by one. Pinching the tips of my fingers, my ears, and my lips, I imagined I was an octopus with crab-claws or some eight-handed pinching monster to acknowledge the obvious lack of blood circulation (or was that blood returning?) all over my poor body. Swimming against the current would have meant ignoring the prickles and running out to buy nicotine.

Now imagine that you were in the desert, hot, and desperately thirsty; you can see water shimmering all around you, but it's a mirage. It's 115 degrees and you would die for a drink of water. Now substitute cigarettes for the water images. Literally, I had smoker's mirages—a lone cigarette surely was in my desk drawer, or underneath my car seat, or in a coat pocket, or somewhere. Nope. Just a whacked-out mirage! But I recognized the hallucination for what it was, and so I successfully swam with the current of quitting.

If you've ever been disoriented and dizzy for any reason and for any length of time, you'll have an appreciation for my constant falling up the stairs and tripping on my own heels, or else falling onto walls as I walked through office hallways. I behaved like a drunken mess while I was quitting. So instead of blaming myself for my discombobulation, I began enjoying the idea that I could be drunk without a drop of alcohol. How cool is that! And I kept on being dizzy for *free!*

Finally, while dealing with the strange need to have a stick between my fingers, I annoyed people by popping my lips and occasionally letting out a whoosh of clean *invisible* air for what should have been smoke. Thus I have never smoked again. I swam with the current and lived.

SURVIVAL HINTS

1. Be prepared for physical symptoms when you quit so that you won't be surprised by them. These include tingling in your hands and feet, a lack of coordination, and hallucinations.
2. Remember, even though it's hard to quit, it will be over before you know it, so hang in there and swim with the tide!

Smokey the Chair

Brian Bowles

BY MY WATCH, it's been five years, two months, two days, thirty-eight minutes, and twenty-two seconds since the day I gave up butts. Yeah, I am still counting. I was a social smoker mostly. Whenever we had company, or went out; whenever I talked; you know: social. A pack some days, sometimes three. If we were drinking, it could even tally up to four packs on a good night.

No matter what we were doing or where we were, my favorite smoking place had always been my old recliner in the den. I loved that chair. It was smoky grey leather that was worn thin, but I loved it anyway. And if they ever held a competition for the most comfortable chair, "Ole Smokey" would have been in the running for first place.

My wife, Eleanor, despised that chair and had been trying to get rid of it for years. I had even caught her once trying to drag it out the door, but luckily for Smokey he was wide in the beam, and no matter how hard Eleanor pushed, she just couldn't get him out. She didn't see me watching her from behind the bushes, but I sat and laughed as she sweat and swore, pushed and tugged, all to no avail. Looking back, I really wish I had taken a picture—not of my crazy wife, but of my Smokey.

Five years ago, Eleanor and the kids pushed me into quitting smoking. Together, they planned the whole thing, an intervention of sorts. After years of listening to me go on about quitting, they decided it was time. And I sort of agreed. Everything I did that required any effort made me short of breath, and I didn't like the limitations this was causing me.

So their first order of smoke-ending business was to change everything that they felt made me want to light up. And that included getting rid of Smokey. It was garbage day, and I had gone on a bakery run for some fresh hard rolls. Upon my return, I saw the garbage truck pulling away from the curb in front of my home. Unconcerned, I waited until the truck was out of the way, then pulled into my driveway.

But when I went inside, I was in for a shock. Ole Smokey was gone, and in his place sat a big, ugly, shiny new recliner. My family stood waiting for my reaction. "How do you like it?" Eleanor asked. "Like it?" I said. "Where's Smokey?" "I thought you needed a new chair. That old piece of garbage has seen its day," she replied.

Garbage was the key word here. Eleanor had thrown my chair into the garbage! Panic set in as I ran from the house to the car. I chased the garbage man down on the street. Upon reaching him, I saw one of the most horrible sights of my life: Smokey sitting straight up in the back of the truck, about to be dumped upon. With its machine arms, the truck had hooked a dumpster and was dangling it in midair. I screamed and yelled, but the driver couldn't hear me. I stood back, horrified, and watched as poor old Smokey was showered with someone else's trash.

I needed a cigarette, but now I was also longing for Smokey. A week or two went by before I would even sit in the new chair. But in time I did, and it wasn't so bad. It wasn't the same, either, because I wasn't smoking; I was just sitting. The new chair took on a new meaning for me. Rather than being my smoking chair, it was my nonsmoking chair. And I must admit that instead of smelling like stale old smoke, it smelled of fresh new leather, a pleasing aroma.

Although I still rub it in with my family about how they tortured me by throwing my chair away, I think the removal of Smokey helped me give up cigarettes. Sometimes just removing yourself from familiar habits can be the edge you need to save your sanity. Five years, two months, two days, forty-eight minutes, two seconds, and counting!

SURVIVAL HINTS

1. Minor changes can provide major results when you're trying to quit smoking. It can be as simple as just changing your daily routine.
2. Keep track of how long it's been since you last smoked. You deserve to brag a little.

The Missing Links:
My Smoking Triggers

Emilia Harung

QUITTING SMOKING can be compared to slamming
your hand in a car door, being bitten by the meanest
of dogs, or torturing yourself just for the heck of it.
When I became pregnant with my first child, I knew I
had to give up smoking. I was a two-pack-a-day smoker
who had failed at several previous attempts to quit.
But this time it wasn't for me—it was for my daughter,
and I knew that somehow I had to do it.

The day I found out I was pregnant was the day I
quit. There was no question about it: I could not

under any circumstance justify poisoning an unborn child. It wasn't easy to do, but I did it—cold turkey. I managed to stop smoking for thirteen months. And for the entire thirteen months, I wanted a cigarette. But for the sake of my child, and ultimately my own, I stuck it out.

For our first night out after the baby was born, my husband and I went to this racetrack for dinner and drinks and some light gambling. I had visited the track many times when I was still a smoker. That night, we ate and gambled, won and lost. That's when my craving for a cigarette became unbearable and I gave in. After thirteen months of torturing myself, I put myself right back to where I had started.

What I didn't realize until that night was that I had always smoked when I was gambling and drinking. And by putting myself back into those surroundings, I had fatally weakened my ability to resist smoking again.

But now I had found the missing link—one that had previously eluded me. I didn't realize how much the desire to smoke came from habits that are linked together, such as horse racing, betting, and smoking. I fell off the carton wagon that night, but I have never smoked again, because I had finally made the connection.

I also found that alcohol was a major trigger. You drink, you smoke. Now, I haven't completely given up drinking, but I have changed my drink preference, which seems to work for me. Sometimes, just altering a situation a bit will get you the results you need.

SURVIVAL HINTS

1. Identify places that trigger your desire to smoke, and then stay away from them.
2. Identify activities that you ordinarily combine with smoking and substitute a different companion activity. For example, if you drink coffee and smoke, switch to tea for a while, or else drink it in a different place than usual, say the living room instead of the kitchen, to help you break the association.
3. For many more smoking cessation hints, visit www.QuitSmoking.com and the Web site for the American Cancer Society, www.cancer.org.

The Smoker's Den

Panchita Morales

I WAS A SMOKER, and a heavy one at that. Anywhere between two to three packs a day was average for me. My husband was also a smoker, although a lighter one than I. Now I had probably been smoking for twenty years, and was promising to quit for at least ten, when we purchased our first home. It was built to suit—to suit us, that is. I had chosen everything, right down to the molding that would border the countertops. If we were going to invest this much money, it was going to be done exactly the way I wanted. The house turned out beautifully, and the time had come to move in.

Once in the house and proclaiming myself on my way to being smoke free, I made a new rule: "No Smoking Allowed." I was not about to yellow our new walls and curtains and poison the place with the foul odor of cigarette smoke. Instead, the front porch became our new smoking den.

In the summer, smoking on the porch is actually pleasant because you get some much needed fresh air. The winter, however, is a different story. One day, during a rather nasty snowstorm—you know the kind, one part snow, one part ice cube, one part freezing rain, and a wind that will literally knock you down if you aren't bracing yourself—I was out on the smoking porch, puffing away as quickly as I could to get my nic-fix before I froze to death, all the while being beaten upon by quarter-sized chunks of hail. It was at that moment I realized that smoking just wasn't worth this abuse. If anyone had seen what I was going through just to be able to smoke, they would have thought me insane.

Cigarettes, I thought to myself, have controlled my life for the very last time. My smoking had decreased by about half in the winter because I dreaded going outside to smoke. Instead of trying to limit the number of cigarettes I was smoking, which had never worked for me, I had limited the places where I could smoke. That, by itself, had cut down the number of cigarettes I smoked in cold weather. My consumption had gone from two or more packs a day to less than one. I realized that if I could cut my smoking in half this easily, I could actually quit altogether. I kept adding limitations into my plan—until one day I no longer smoked. It took me almost three seasons, but I succeeded. And I have been smoke free now for more than two years.

SURVIVAL HINTS

1. You must want to quit before making an attempt; otherwise, it won't work for you.
2. Take a good hard look at why you smoke, and then try to address those reasons so that they won't derail your efforts to quit smoking.
3. Determine when and where you smoke the least, and increase the amount of time doing those things or being in those places. Doing so will help you stop altogether.

The Misbehavin' Cravin'

Melanie Gibbs

I'VE GOT A MISBEHAVING CRAVING that acts up every time the word "smoking" comes up. My mind misbehaves and my body craves. It could be as simple as the slightest whiff of another's bad habit or a poison-yourself advertisement that just happens to catch my eye. A Marlboro or a Camel will do while I'm down and out in Newport. Hell, anything will do. A rolled-up weed would succeed.

I quit smoking more than ten years ago, but not without a fight. I was a slave to my cigarettes. They ruled my life. I always had to make sure I had enough to get through the night and the morning pot of coffee. Oh, that's the worst, a full pot of coffee and only one cigarette. Talk about frightening. It was downright ruinous. One day, I even went so far as to throw on my trench coat over my pink pajamas—just to run to the convenience store to get a pack of butts to smoke while enjoying my second addiction, which, of course, is my coffee. I'm not really sure what's worse: running out of smokes or running out of coffee, but I managed to do both several times.

This particular day was no exception. Now, you would think I could have at least gotten dressed to go to the store, but I had a thing about wearing clean clothes on an unshowered body. Now that I look back, I had a "thing" about many things. Smoking was my vice. I smoked in the morning, in the car on the way to work, and after meals and snacks; even the smell of food made me smoke. I smoked before a shower, after a shower, and, if I could have figured out a way to do it, I even would have smoked *in* the shower.

So here I am standing in line at the counter in my pink jammies, sneakers, and trench coat, waiting for my smokes, when this seedy looking juvenile delinquent strolls in, looking like trouble, maybe thinking he's going to knock off the store for a couple of bucks.

Now not only had I not had a smoke this morning, but at this point I also hadn't had a cup of coffee. Those of you who share these same addictions know the mood such deprivation can cause. I was on edge, to put it mildly. The punk had moved in front of me to make his demands, obviously thinking the ruffled looking one in the pink jammies wasn't a threat to him.

But all I could think of was the delays that the little misbehaving dirtball was about to cause to my morning coffee- and cigarette-craving routine. If he got away with robbing the store, I would have to stay there for hours talking to the cops about what I had seen and heard. There was no way I was about to let that happen.

On my right, I noticed a stand full of wooden-handled umbrellas. Without a second thought, I grabbed the closest and biggest one. Swinging it like a bat, I blasted the little creep right upside the head, dropping him to the floor like a tree falling in the forest. Down he went. Out cold.

The cops came and arrested him, and I had pretty much put the incident out of my mind until that night when I saw myself on the news. The store had released the video film of the whole episode. There I was in my pink jammies, knocking out one of the world's finest dirtbags without batting an eye.

I sat back that night and thought about what I had done and why. It was a potentially dangerous move, and the guy could have been armed. But I was temporarily insane. Between the lack of nicotine and the lack of caffeine, my common sense had gone out the window. I knew I had to get a grip. So now I do not refer to that day as the day of the attempted robbery; instead, it's the day I smoked my last cigarette. I'm still addicted to coffee, but you gotta live!

SURVIVAL HINTS

1. Smokers often find themselves using nicotine as a stress reducer. If stress is one of your reasons for smoking, look for coping alternatives.
2. Physical activity is one of the best-known stress reducers. Take up walking, jogging, or playing tennis.
3. Seek out stress-management groups in your area to keep you from smoking again when you're getting too tense.

The Smoking Diet

Jacob C. Katz

WHAT IS IT about quitting smoking that can turn a sane individual into a crazed lunatic? Why do the words "I'm quitting" instill an instant craving to smoke into your brain? Why do nonsmokers always feel the need to help you along your path to nonsmoking hell? Why is it we always want what we can't have?

Quitting smoking can be compared to being on a diet. The Smoking Diet. You may not be giving up chocolate cake, but you are still giving up something your body desires, making your brain work overtime and your cravings increase to uncontrollable levels.

Because most of the problems with quitting are in your mind, maybe the most appropriate way to give up cigarettes is to put yourself on the Smoking Diet. Tell yourself you're not quitting smoking cigarettes, you're just going on a smoking diet. If you take it day by day, it may be slightly easier.

Notice that I said slightly. I'm a smoker and I know it's not easy. I quit many times before I quit for good. In the end, I did it one day at a time. I also told no one of my efforts while attempting this horrible feat. Eventually they noticed, but even that took time. Quitting is a day-by-day chore, like giving up drinking, and until I know I will never smoke again, I am just a smoker on the Smoking Diet.

SURVIVAL HINTS

1. Although quitting is the first step, maintaining your "quit" status is the second step.
2. Whenever you feel the urge to smoke you should focus on your reasoning for quitting, remind yourself of the time and effort you have put into it already, and think about the improvements you've already made in your life and everyone else's around you.
3. Wait out the desire to give in and smoke; it will pass.

Resources

American Cancer Society
1-800-ACS-2345
www.cancer.org

American Heart Association
1 800-242-1793 (call center) or 800-242-1793
www.amhrt.org

American Lung Association
1-800-586-4872 or 212-315-8700
www.lungusa.org

National Cancer Institute
Cancer Information Service
1-800-4-CANCER or 800-422-6237
www.cancer.gov

Office on Smoking & Health Centers for Disease Control and Prevention
770-448-5705
www.cdc.gov/tobacco

Tobacco Information & Prevention Source (TIPS) National Center for Chronic Disease Prevention and Health Promotion
www.cdc.gov/tobacco/quit/canquit.htm

Nicotine Anonymous
1-877-TRY-NICA (1-877-879-6422)
www.nicotine-anonymous.org

Smokefree.gov
Online materials, including information on state Quitlines
www.smokefree.gov

Foundation for a Smoke Free America
www.anti-smoking.org/quitting.htm

Quitnet.com
This is the original Internet site for quitting, which is associated with the Boston University School of Public Health.
www.quitnet.com

QuitSmoking.com
One of the best sites, includes chat board for smoking cessation support.
www.quitsmoking.com

WhyQuit.com
Specifically for those who want to quit cold turkey, this site is packed with information and helpful suggestions.
www.whyquit.com

Online Stop Smoking Guide
Free educational materials on this site sponsored by the San Francisco Internet Health Research Center, University of California, San Francisco.
www.stopsmoking.ucsf.edu

ConsumerHealthDigest.com
Provides advice and the top ten Smoking Cessation Products on the market today.
http://consumerhealthdigest.com/smokecessation. htm?source=google/2ROTAD

Quitting Smoking, FamilyDoctor.org
This site is "operated by the American Academy of Family Physicians (AAFP), a national medical organization representing more than 93,700 family physicians, family practice residents and medical students. All of

the information on this site has been written and reviewed by physicians and patient education professionals at the AAFP."
http://familydoctor.org/x5158.xml

Quit Smoking Help Review Site
Evaluates the effectiveness of all the quit-smoking products on the market through user voting system. Includes verified user quotes.
http://quit-smoking-help.org/

You Can Quit Smoking
Office of the Surgeon General, U.S. Government
http://www.surgeongeneral.gov/tobacco/
consquits.htm

Quit.org
Very helpful site based in Australia.
www.quit.org.au/index2.html

Giving Up Smoking
Advice and suggestions from the British National Health Service.
http://www.givingupsmoking.co.uk/home/

So You Wanna Quit Smoking
Provides information on various methods of quitting smoking.
www.soyouwanna.com/site/syws/quit/quit.html

Acknowledgments

First of all the authors would like to acknowledge our wonderful editor, Marnie Cochran, executive editor at Da Capo Press, for instantly getting it when we first called to talk about our idea for the Staying Sane series. From the beginning, Marnie understood what we were trying to do, and she has helped us immeasurably in making our vision for the series take shape. Even though we probably have driven her a little crazy sometimes, we hope she'll stay sane through it all and for a long time to come! Thank you, Marnie, for everything we know you do for us, along with all the things we never even hear about. We both know how lucky we are to have our series in your capable hands.

Next, we wish to thank all the other members of the Da Capo Press staff for their hard work on this book: Alexis Rizzuto, assistant editor; John Radziewicz, editorial director; Liz Tzetzo, director of sales; and Erica Lawrence, production editor.

Finally, and most important, we wish to thank our contributors, especially Ed Fitzgerald, Tony Vlamis, Joyce Romano, Ellen P. Sander, Peter Mastracchio, P. J. Dempsey, Kyle Ezell, Theo Pollack, Janice Kuta, and Dralyn Veech, all successful quitters with great, funny stories that will encourage and inspire anyone who wants to join their ranks.